Ginette Watson

The Official Cub Scout Annual
of the Scout Association

Scouts

Edited by Sara Fielding
and Mike Brennan

Contents

This book belongs to:

of the

Cub Scout Pack

£4.50

Shere Khan the tiger thought he had young Mowgli within his grasp. See if you can help Mowgli to get back to the safety of Akela without crossing any black lines in the jungle. Beware you don't lead him into the clutches of Kaa, the evil one.

Check your answer on page 61.

THE APPLIANCE OF SCIENCE!!

photographs by Ron Crabb

The Science Museum in London is crammed full of exciting exhibits from the world of science and technology and William, Alan, Ronan, Jeremy, Simon and Bryn from the 8th Wimbledon Cub Scout Pack visited it to find out more.

Situated in South Kensington, London SW7, the Science Museum is next-door-neighbour to the Natural History Museum and a convenient five minute walk from Baden-Powell House, ideal for Cub Scout Packs who are visiting London to either stay at or pop into on the way to the museum.

So, after a quick look around Baden-Powell House – and some huge plates of chips for lunch in the Baden-Powell House restaurant! – the 8th Wimbledon were ready to whizz around the Science Museum and see as much as they could.

It was certainly a good thing that the Cub Scouts were full of energy, as plenty is needed to tramp around the Science Museum's vast floors, all covering different themes and showing various stages of industrial and scientific development. It is practically impossible to see everything the museum has to offer in just one day so the Cub Scouts decided to look at the sections of the museum which they found most interesting, and save the rest for another day!

The Exploration of SPACE

On their way to another floor of the museum, the Cub Scouts stopped for a quick look at a huge mill engine dating back to 1903 which came from Harle Syke Mill in Burnley and was used to drive 1700 spinning looms.

Moving swiftly along, another fascinating area of the museum revealed what transport used to be like back in the olden days and the 8th Wimbledon found themselves whisked back in time as they were hailed by a 'real old-fashioned' conductor who invited them on a guided tour of a Corporation Tramcar. The Cub Scouts loved this taste of history as they were able to really join in and enjoy the mini-drama.

On the ground floor of the museum they found the Exploration of Space exhibition, a fascinating display of real and model spacecraft and rockets. This exhibition traces the historical and technological background of space exploration from earliest times to the present day, and beyond. Three main questions are raised and answered for visitors – What are rockets and satellites? How do they work? What do they do? The Cub Scouts spent some time finding out some of the answers and trying out some of the computer challenges, such as designing a rocket.

An exciting part of the exhibition is Apollo 10, the actual craft in which three astronauts orbited the Moon in May 1969. Equally interesting is the replica of Apollo 11 LEM (Lunar Excursion Module) which took two Apollo astronauts down onto the Moon in July 1969.

(The tramcar is a Glasgow Corporation Tramcar No 585 which was built between 1901–2 and is an electrically driven version of the company's earlier 'horse-drawn' tramcar.)

(There were many of these engines built in the late nineteenth to the early twentieth century to provide power for industry. There was a decline in their use from the 1930s onward due to an increase in the use of electrical motors.)

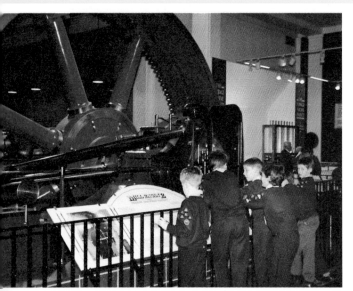

(The London Transport Tube Car No 3327 which ran 1½ million miles during its 32 year service.)

The next stop was a little further into the future – a London Transport Tube Car which was put into service in 1929 for use on the Piccadilly line. The Cub Scouts enjoyed spotting the differences between this Tube Car and the more modern version that they had travelled on earlier!

Another favourite the boys found in the transport section of the museum was a Morris Mini Minor which has been opened up to show in cross-section what the engine and other working parts look like. Great fun for pretending to drive or even wheel away!

On the first floor of the Science Museum, the Cubs found the gallery that all children (and adults!) absolutely love. Called Launch Pad, it consists of experiments and demonstrations and is the museum's hands-on technology experience. The idea is to learn about technology in a fun and enjoyable way by providing experiments that are like games and challenges. It was hard work trying to tear the Cub Scouts away from Launch Pad to see some more of the museum!

(A Morris Mini Minor which was launched in August 1959, born of the need for fuel economy following the Suez crisis of 1956.)

Next on the list was the Food for Thought exhibition at the Sainsbury gallery which covers everything anyone could ever need or want to know about food. It even has its own McDonalds restaurant which the Cubs made a bee-line for! No real burgers, unfortunately, but plenty of information on the background of burgers and fast food. The Cub Scouts loved it and had plenty of fun pretending to order everything on the menu anyway! Apart from the fun aspects of the Food for Thought exhibition, there is plenty to see and learn about what we need from food, how it is made and what we buy, sell and eat.

Of course, all the thinking about food made the boys feel quite peckish so they headed for some quick refreshments in a cafeteria set in the background of what seemed to be an aeroplane hangar – the museum's impressive collection of aircraft from various points in history. Feeling refreshed the Cubs strolled through for a look at the magnificent 'planes and then hurried off to get a quick look at the Lego exhibition – time was running out!

A stroke of luck was that during our visit the Lego Motor Show was being held with an exhibition of seventeen scaled down model cars crafted entirely from Lego! Probably the Cub Scouts' favourite half hour of their day was spent digging deep into the 'Motor Make' section's sunken pit which was filled with Lego. You just sit around the edge and dig in!

Unfortunately, it was nearly time to go and so with a quick final glance around, the Cub Scouts made tracks back home.

As is evident, there is an extraordinary amount to see and do at the Science Museum and the constantly changing exhibitions as well as the old favourites which always remain, mean that it is a place most people will enjoy a visit to given the opportunity. The 8th Wimbledon Cub Scout Pack certainly did it justice and went home asking their Akela, 'When can we go again?'

The Lego Motor show ended in March 1991

The Editors of the 1992 Cub Scout Annual would like to express their thanks to all the staff at the Science Museum for their help and co-operation with this feature.

Fabulous Beasts & Incredible Creatures

Do you believe in monsters? I don't mean dinosaurs, which everybody knows were real, and I don't mean the kind that hide under your bed or in your closet, which everybody knows aren't real. I mean the kind in between, the monsters of myths and legends from long, long ago.

Legends are traditional stories usually told about famous people or events with a slight distortion of truth. As the legends are passed on from generation to generation, the stories become more and more exaggerated and more fantastic until they reach a point where they become unbelievable. Myths, on the other hand, are purely fictional although the characters and events are often loosely based on real people and events. The ancient Greeks are particularly noted for their mythology.

Below and on pages 23, 39 and 49 are some of the most well-known monsters and mythological creatures. There is no evidence that any of them ever really existed, but it would be nice to believe that, perhaps, some of the friendlier ones did, at one time, walk the earth . . .

CENTAUR

According to Greek legend the centaurs were a race of creatures who were half man and half horse and dwelt in the plains of Thessaly. They were noted for being a rather unruly and riotous lot, a bit like today's football fans. The earliest representations of Centaurs were excavated near Famagusta in Cyprus in 1962 and were thought to date back to around 1800 B.C.

CYCLOPS

In Greek mythology this was a race of one-eyed giants who lived in Sicily. Like the centaurs, this lot were also a bunch of savages and survived by eating flocks of sheep and goats. When the stocks of sheep and goats ran out the Cyclops were known to eat each other!

SIGNING AND BRAILLE

As a Cub Scout you will be familiar with lots of different forms of communication. The obvious ones — speech and the written word — may be transmitted using telephones, facsimile machines (FAX), radio, television, etc. You may also have come across such methods as Semaphore and Morse Code.

You are less likely to have come across the two methods of communication featured here, although both are very important to a great deal of people all over the world.

Braille

The determination of a young child to overcome his handicap after being blinded in an accident when he was three years old resulted in the invention of a means of communication which would change the lives of many people suffering from blindness.

In 1829, Louis Braille (1809–52) invented the special alphabet system made up of raised dots which enables blind people to 'read'. Today, apart from use in the transcription of books, braille has also been adapted for use on domestic appliances and technical equipment. It has helped blind people to become self sufficient and has enabled many to take up a wide range of careers which would otherwise have been very difficult to accomplish.

A	B	C	D	E	F	G	H	I	J

K	L	M	N	O	P	Q	R	S	T

U	V	W	X	Y	Z	and	for	the	with

of	Oblique stroke		Numeral sign	Poetry sign	Apostrophe sign	Hyphen		Dash

Lower signs	,	;	:	.	!	()	?/" "	,,

Sign language

Sign language, as used in this country, comes in two forms. One, as shown, is purely a manual alphabet in which both hands are used to represent a letter. You can see how each symbol forms, or at least suggests, the letter it represents.

The other form, again using both hands, is made up of a series of actions which represent words, phrases and sometimes whole sentences.

These methods of communication are particularly useful to people with impaired hearing and/or speech impediments. Deaf people are often very good lip-readers, thus someone communicating with a deaf person will usually make use of sign language whilst, at the same time, speaking the words.

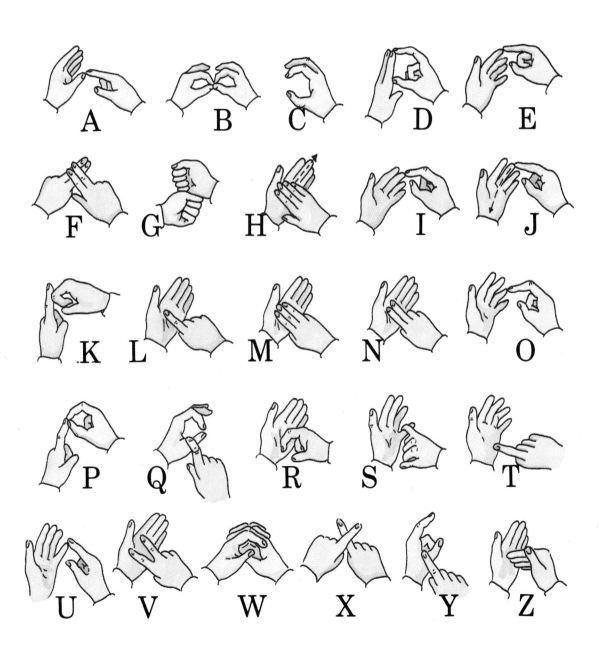

Worms

Some astonishing worm facts!

★ It has been estimated that in some areas of the country a good piece of pasture-land can have a worm population of 3 million worms per acre.

★ Every year worms recycle ten tonnes of new soil over every acre of land.

★ It is believed that the stones of Stonehenge are sinking at a rate of about 15cm (6 inches) per century due to worm activity.

★ During times of drought, an earthworm will burrow 30 metres (60 feet) into the ground in search of water.

Most people think of worms as horrible, slimy, squidgy things that live in the garden and are only good for catching fish and being eaten by birds. This is mostly true – worms *are* horrible, slimy, squidgy things that live in the garden – BUT they are also very interesting creatures that play an important part in keeping our gardens and fields healthy.

Worms come in all different types and sizes with some growing up to 3.6 metres (12 ft) in length! Fortunately, these 'monsters' are only found in Australia; the worm you are most likely to come across in Britain, the earthworm, is tiny in comparison, the longest being about 30cm (12 inches) in length.

Most earthworms are a pinky purple or bluish brown colour and their bodies are made up of numerous (usually between 75 and 250) rings or segments. Each segment has a few short bristles which are very difficult to see but can be felt if you rub your finger along the worm. These bristles help the worm to move along. The front end of the worm stretches forward and gets thinner as it does so. The bristles on the front segments of the worm then grip the earth and the worm draws along the rest of its body stage by stage. This works very well on ordinary ground but is completely useless on smooth surfaces, as the bristles cannot get a good grip. The bristles also come in handy for holding the worms safely in their burrows. If you have ever seen a bird struggling to pull a worm out of the ground you will know how well this works.

Earthworms keep our gardens healthy by burrowing in the soil, letting in air and water which are particularly good for the roots of plants and help them to grow. Worms also keep the soil fertile by eating tiny pieces of dead plants mixed with soil. This waste passes through the worm's body and is deposited as small, fertile lumps of soil known as 'worm casts'. If you get a chance, have a look and see if you can find some worm casts in your garden or in a local park or field.

how worms move

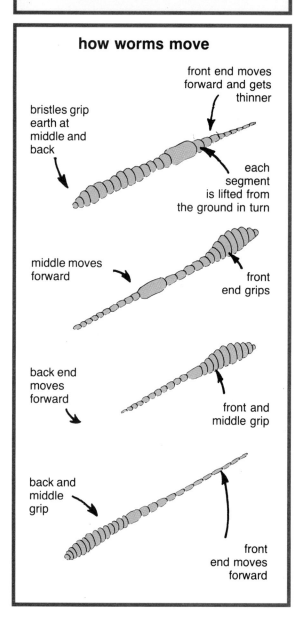

bristles grip earth at middle and back

front end moves forward and gets thinner

each segment is lifted from the ground in turn

middle moves forward

front end grips

back end moves forward

front and middle grip

back and middle grip

front end moves forward

Build your own worm farm

If you are interested in finding out more about worms the best way to do it is to build your own worm farm and study them yourself. Any good sized glass (or clear plastic) container will do but an old fish tank, or large sweet jar, is ideal. If your container has a lid, remember to make some holes in it to allow air to get in.

Cover the bottom of the container with a layer of damp soil from your garden, to a depth of about 5cm (2 inches) and cover the layer of soil with a layer of sand about 2.5cm (1 inch) deep. Repeat this, adding layers of soil and sand until the container is about three-quarters full. When you have done this, mark the positions of the layers with a felt-tip marker pen or by taping a strip of paper to the container and marking the layers on that.

Now you have to find some worms. The best way to do this is to dig up a few spadefuls of soil shortly after it has been raining, as this brings the worms nearer to the surface. It might be worth asking an adult to help you with the digging. Once you have found your worms remember that, as with all living creatures, you should treat them with respect and handle them carefully. The idea of picking a worm up probably doesn't appeal to you very much, but although they look pretty ugly, once you have held one you will be surprised by the fact that holding a worm is not quite as unpleasant as you may have imagined. When you have found about six worms carefully place them in your farm.

Leave some small scraps of food on top of the soil, eg cheese, some vegetables, bits of plants, leaves, etc. Don't overdo it because you want to be able to see which types of food the worms eat.

Keep the worms for just under a week and study them daily to see what happens. In particular, watch what happens to the layers of soil and sand, and to the food you have left. After a couple of days you should be able to find some worm casts on the surface of the soil.

When you have finished studying the worms, carefully return them to where you found them. Try to do this in the evening when it is cooler and there is less chance of birds coming along and eating them.

Keep a record of your worm studies; perhaps you could use this project as part of your Scientist Activity Badge.

WORM FARM

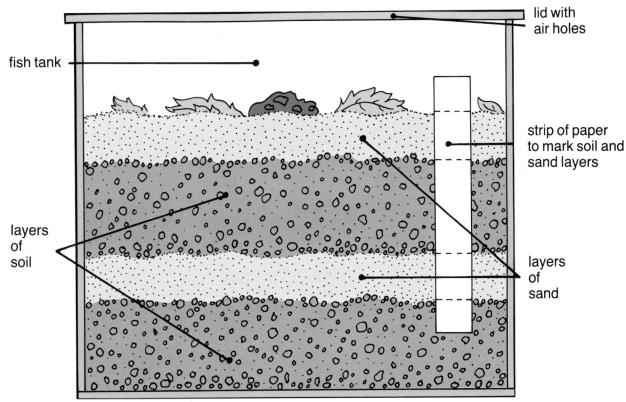

lid with air holes

fish tank

strip of paper to mark soil and sand layers

layers of soil

layers of sand

SPACE EXPLORERS

PT. 1 the Country CODE

ART: Steve Harman.

CLIFF BROWN'S PUZZLE PAGE

What are the Activity Badges?

Join the dots and you will be able to name them.

Check your answers on page 61.

Find the Words of the Cub Scout Law

They are all hidden in the picture (that's 19 words!).

Billy and the Friendly Ghost

By Neil Williams

The only sounds that could be heard in Room 44 of Baden-Powell House were alarm clocks ticking the minutes away to morning, seven Cub Scouts snoring, and one Cub Scout sobbing. Billy felt very unhappy. Although he had only joined the Cub Scouts four weeks ago, he had begged and pleaded with his parents to let him take up the spare place on the weekend to London that Akela had organized for his Pack, as he had really wanted to be with all his new friends. Also, Akela had said that it would be nice for Billy to be invested in London as a special treat, but now Billy wasn't so sure that Cub Scouting was for him after all.

The problem was, the Promise and Law seemed so hard to keep and Billy knew that it wasn't going to be easy living up to such high standards. And as for knots! Well, he couldn't get the hang of knotting no matter how hard he tried.

Billy rubbed the tears from his eyes and decided to get up and go for a little walk. He didn't want any of his friends to wake up and ask him what the matter was. He would feel silly if his friends were to see him crying. Creeping past the seven Cub Scouts who were dreaming about the next fun-filled and action-packed day, Billy gently opened the door and slipped out into the quiet, shadowy corridor. He didn't know why but instead of walking along the corridor, he crept down the stairs and went towards the huge oak door of the library, which was standing ajar. The moonlight cast shadows all around. All was quiet and still and yet Billy felt strangely comforted

being in the library, which was a lovely snug room filled with lots of old books and games and glass cases full of really interesting old things that used to belong to Scouts years and years ago. Billy had already spent a long time looking at all the objects in the cases and reading stories of how Scouting used to be in the olden days when lots of Scouts went to a huge camp at a place called Brownsea Island with Baden-Powell, the very first Scout Leader. Billy wandered around the library looking up at the old oil paintings of famous Scouters who seemed to stare back down at him. They all looked very important and a little bit fierce.

Billy curled up in an old armchair in a corner, shivering and beginning once again to feel unhappy and cold and a little bit homesick. He hugged a cushion to himself and laid his head back on the old chair and very soon he began to dream about the camp at Brownsea Island, imagining that he was there, listening to Baden-Powell telling a story all about how to be a good Scout. Suddenly, a voice came out of the shadows and Billy strained to see in the gloom. He could see an elderly man sitting in a nearby armchair and although it was very dark, Billy thought his face looked clever and kind.

His voice was deep, rich and reassuring as he said, 'So, what seems to be the problem?'

Billy felt his voice wobble a bit but he managed to say, 'I'm scared that I'll never be a good Cub Scout.'

'I see,' replied the man, 'and why is that?'

then, quick as a flash, were undone again and oh, Billy was enchanted. He never realized that knots could be so much fun! Then, slowly and carefully, the old man showed Billy how to do a Reef Knot, probably the most useful knot of all and very easy to do, especially with a bit of practice. The old man's fingers weaved in and out to create the knot and then he took Billy step by step through the same process. At first, Billy still couldn't get it right but with patience the old man worked with him, over and over again.

Gradually Billy began to get the hang of it and as he practised, he listened, fascinated by the old man's stories of his adventures in far away lands.

A long time later, Billy's new friend, noticing the little boy's eyes beginning to droop, smiled and said gently, 'There, you see, you've done it, a perfect Reef Knot.'

Billy smiled too, for there in his hand was, indeed, a Reef Knot.

'Time for bed I think,' said the old man. 'Keep my bit of string and practise your knots as often as possible. You'll soon wonder why you were ever worried about them at all.'

Slowly, Billy began to tell his tale of how he felt anxious and frightened that he couldn't keep the Law and Promise and how he was so worried that he couldn't get to grips with knotting. In fact, he hadn't yet managed to learn a single one. All the time the man listened quietly and as Billy told him all his worries he began to feel much calmer and not so frightened about it all.

'Well now,' said the kind old man, 'maybe I can reassure you. Let's start with the Promise. Those words make up a personal set of guidelines so that instead of following the crowd you can make up your own mind and be ready to accept responsibility. Those words tell you people may need your help and that you have to share and care for others and recognize that their lives are just as important as your own. The words remind you that this world is God's creation and that he has entrusted its care to you. You must help to look after and protect the environment for future generations.'

Billy nodded slowly in agreement. This was a much clearer way of looking at the Promise.

The old man continued. 'Now, I'll try and show you how much fun knotting can be, so that once you practise a little bit you'll enjoy showing your friends lots of tricks as well as knowing how to do all the important knots that are so useful for all kinds of things.'

The old man took a length of string from his pocket and began to show Billy lots of wonderful tricks. His fingers moved nimbly through the air and he produced knots that vanished, knots that looped into magic circles around his fingers and

'I'm not so scared of becoming a Cub Scout now,' Billy yawned, sleepily, 'thanks to you.'

At the door to Room 44, he turned to wave to his new friend, but there was no one there. Billy crept quietly in and was soon fast asleep.

When he woke the next morning, Billy rushed down to breakfast to tell all his friends and Akela about his adventure the night before.

'I'm sorry to hear that you didn't sleep well, Billy,' said Akela, 'but are you sure that you didn't just drop off to sleep in the library and dream your adventure?'

'No,' Billy protested, 'I really did meet him and I think he lives here in Baden-Powell House. Look, there is his picture,' he said, pointing at one of the large portraits hanging on the wall.

'Now I know you must have been dreaming,' Akela smiled kindly. 'That is a portrait of Baden-Powell himself, the Founder of the Scout Movement. He's been dead for a long time now, Billy.'

'But it was him,' Billy protested again, adding quietly, 'I know it was.'

When breakfast was finished, Billy walked slowly back along the corridor to his room and just as he was opening the door he spotted something lying on the carpet. He bent down to pick it up, his heart pounding. It was his Reef Knot! He must have dropped it last night when he was so sleepy. He was glad that he'd found it because his friend, the old man, had told him to take care of it and he had a feeling that it was going to come in very useful for him once he was invested as a Cub Scout.

Back in his room, Billy pulled on his Cub Scout sweatshirt, bare at the moment, but one day it would be full of badges, he just knew it would. Excited and happy and now, looking forward to his Investiture Ceremony later that morning, he rushed out of his room and stopped in his tracks. At the far end of the corridor stood his new friend. Now Billy could clearly see that it was, indeed, Baden-Powell, his face so warm and kind. Billy started to speak but the old man signalled silence.

'Good luck,' he called and gravely saluted the latest recruit.

'Billy, where are you?' called Akela's voice from down at the bottom of the staircase.

Billy turned for a split second towards the sound of Akela's voice, then he turned to salute in return, but there was no one there. So smiling to himself and still clutching his Reef Knot, he went to be invested and to make his Cub Scout Promise feeling very special indeed.

GET (UN) Knotted

Knot tying is one of the most basic and important parts of Cub Scouting and any Cub Scout worth his woggle will be familiar with how to tie a reef knot, a bowline, a sheet bend and a highwayman's hitch. If you have ever looked through a book of knots you may have been overwhelmed by the number of knots there are, but excluding decorative knots there are actually only six types of knot. These are:

i) The knot for tying the ends together;
ii) The knot for tying two ropes together;
iii) The knot for tying a rope to a post;
iv) Making a loop in a rope;
v) Shortening a rope or taking up the slack;
vi) A knot in the end of a rope.

During your time as a Cub Scout you will get plenty of opportunities to learn and try out some of the more useful knots, particularly the ones used in camping and pioneering. However, if your knot-learning sessions start to become a little tedious you might like to try the following rope tricks (at the end of your knotting session perhaps) to add a little bit of fun. If you master the tricks well enough you could use them in a magic show, maybe as part of your Entertainer Activity Badge or in the Creativity sections of your Adventure or Adventure Crest Awards.

Vanishing Knot (1)

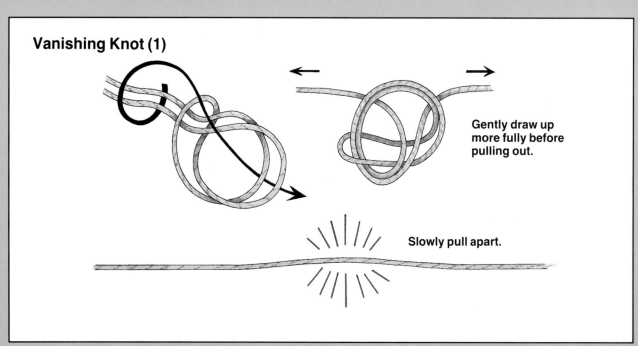

Gently draw up more fully before pulling out.

Slowly pull apart.

Vanishing Knot (2)

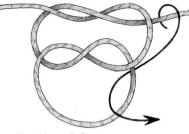

Reef knot left well open

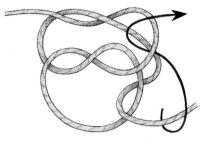

then two more tucks

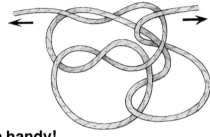

and pull apart.

This one could come in handy! A loop of cord or string is drawn right through your hand.

1: Lay down a loop of cord on a table exactly as above.

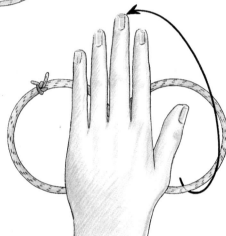

2: Lift the lower part of right-hand loop over the upper part and under the fingers.

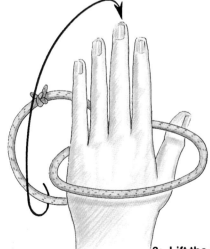

3: Lift the lower part of left-hand loop under its upper part and under the fingers.

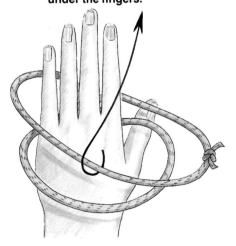

4: Now, just pull up one of the strings on the back of the hand.

The Magic Ring

From a loop suspended from a person's fingers a ring is removed while the loops remain on the fingers.

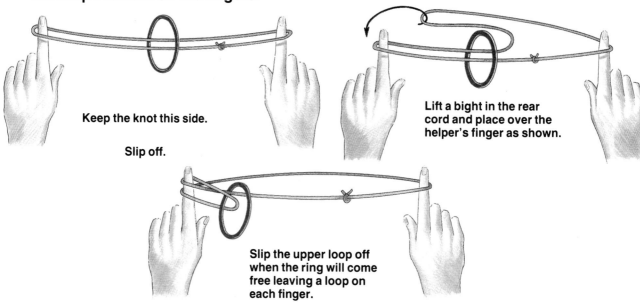

Keep the knot this side.

Slip off.

Lift a bight in the rear cord and place over the helper's finger as shown.

Slip the upper loop off when the ring will come free leaving a loop on each finger.

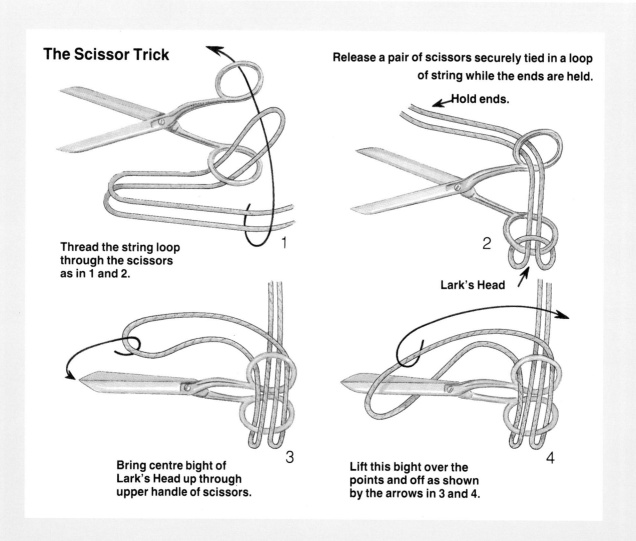

The Scissor Trick

Release a pair of scissors securely tied in a loop of string while the ends are held.

Hold ends.

Thread the string loop through the scissors as in 1 and 2.

1

2

Lark's Head

Bring centre bight of Lark's Head up through upper handle of scissors.

3

Lift this bight over the points and off as shown by the arrows in 3 and 4.

4

GORGON

The gorgons were the three daughters of Phorcys and Ceto and were called Stheno, Euryale and Medusa. They had big claws, enormous teeth and snakes instead of hair. Medusa was the only mortal one of the three and her face was supposed to be so terribly ugly that anybody who looked at it turned to stone. Even after the hero Perseus had killed her by chopping off her head those who were unfortunate to gaze upon her face were still turned to stone.

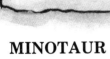

GRIFFIN or GRYPHON

A mythological monster, supposedly the guardian of hidden treasure. The Griffin had the body, tail and hind legs of a lion and the head, forelegs and wings of an eagle. A Griffin can often be found in heraldry and, arguably, the most famous Griffin of all appears on the armorial crest of the City of London. There are also two statues of Griffins on London's Embankment guarding the city's western boundary.

MINOTAUR

In Greek legend the Minotaur was a monster half man, half bull and was supposed to be the offspring of Pasiphae, the wife of King Minos of Crete, and a bull. The Minotaur was kept in a labyrinth from which it could not escape and lived on a diet of youths and maidens sent as an annual tribute from Athens. The Minotaur was slain by Theseus with the aid of King Minos' daughter Ariadne. Theseus found his way out of the labyrinth by following a trail of string which he had laid on his way in.

23

Micro Machines

FROM START TO FINISH

Micro Machine Man

Hey, it's the Micro Machine Man, and I'm here to tell you how Micro Machines are made.

Micro Machines are a range of miniature vehicles and playsets which over the last five years have become one of the most successful collectable vehicle ranges of all time. Since the first vehicle was designed and produced in 1986, over 350 million Micro Machines have been collected worldwide! All vehicles are approximately 3 cm (1¼ inches) long, and if you took all the vehicles produced so far and put them end to end, they would stretch from London to Singapore or from New York to Tokyo. In the UK alone over 20 million vehicles have been collected, enough to stretch from London to Edinburgh, or around the M25 five times! But, no matter how many Micro Machines are produced they all start life the same way. Have you ever wondered how a Micro Machine is actually made? Read on and find out how!

The very first Micro Machines were produced in 1986. Originally there were only 48 different vehicles in the collection. Since then new styles have been constantly added and now over 400 different styles are available. So where does a Micro Machine begin life?

First of all we have to decide what vehicle we want to produce. The most popular motor vehicles from the past, present and prototype cars of the future are studied and only the very best are chosen.

When we have decided what vehicles we want to put into the new vehicle collection, photographs and drawings of the actual vehicles are given to artists. The artist then draws the real vehicle as it would look like as a Micro Machine, experimenting with different colours and styles of decoration. When the final style is decided, the artwork is then passed on to the technical drawing department.

Here exact drawings of every detail of the Micro Machines are made. These drawings have to be very accurate as a mistake here could lead to a situation where a Micro Machine will not fit together when it is produced. To make sure that this will never happen, final technical drawings are given to a model maker who makes proving models. These models are exact replicas of what the final Micro Machine will look like down to the last detail. If there are any mistakes in the drawings it will be found now.

Once everyone is satisfied the drawings are correct they are passed to the mould maker. It takes a lot of skill and experience to make a mould. The moulds are made from blocks of steel out of which the mould maker machines an exact replica of the finished Micro Machine. Many of the moulds have multiple impressions which means up to 10 or even 20 vehicles can be made at a time. When the moulds are completed we are ready to produce the finished Micro Machine.

The newly made mould is loaded onto an injection moulding machine. All the plastic parts of a Micro Machine are made in a process called 'injection moulding'. In this process raw plastic pellets are heated until they become liquid. The liquid plastic is injected into the mould until it is completely full. After a few seconds the plastic solidifies, the mould opens and ejector pins push the Micro Machine body out into collection boxes.

Micro Machine design drawings

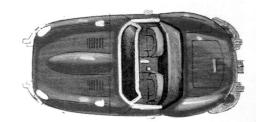

Early stage of design model

These machines are fully automatic. In a large factory hundreds of them work side by side. The machine operators ensure that they do not run out of plastic and the collection boxes are removed when full.

The next stage is decoration. This is done by a combination of spray painting, hand painting and decal application. First of all the vehicle body is completely sprayed with the main body colour and is then left to dry. Drying is aided by passing the vehicles through large heaters. If a second major colour is required, then a spray mask is produced. This mask fits over the Micro Machine vehicle and exposes only the area where the new colour is required. This area is then sprayed and the mask removed. This again is left to dry and the Micro Machine is then passed on for final hand decoration and decal application.

This stage of the manufacturing process is very delicate indeed. Tiny details such as the tail lights, window wipers and door handles are painted by hand using minute paint brushes.

When all the decorations are completed the body is ready for assembly. On the assembly line the chassis and wheels are attached and any other moving parts, i.e. doors and bonnets, are assembled.

At last the Micro Machine is finished and ready for packaging. As Micro Machines are sold in many countries around the world, the factory has to be careful to use the correct language packaging.

Now the collection pack of Micro Machines vehicles is given the final quality control test and if it passes it is ready for the long journey to your local shop.

Undecorated Micro Machine

The pack of vehicles is packed with others into a shipping carton. On the carton is a description of the vehicles, details of when they were made, and the code for the factory. The shipping cartons are loaded into containers and taken by truck to the docks. Most Micro Machines are made in China and they are transported to the United Kingdom by ship. It takes over five weeks for a ship to sail from China to England. When they arrive they are carried to a warehouse by truck and from there by smaller trucks and vans to your local toy shop. Now you can buy them.

So how long do you think it takes to produce a Micro Machine from the initial idea to it arriving in the shops? In fact it takes a full 12 months and the skill and dedication of hundreds of people. We think the effort is worth it, do you?

Now turn the page and enter the Micro Machines Competition.

A complete vehicle

A Micro Machine collection

The Great Micro Machines Competition

You could be the winner of one of these brilliant Micro Machines Race in a Case playsets if you enter our great competition.

The Race in a Case is a fully enclosed Micro Machine racing system packed in a transportable case and includes two high performance Micro Machine slot racing cars, two pistol grip hand controllers and a power pack. There are also roadway and parking areas for your regular Micro Machine vehicles.

We have five Race in a Case sets to give away as First Prizes to the Winners and 20 Runners-up will each receive a pack of 20 Micro Machines. All you have to do to enter is:

Imagine you are one of the design team at Micro Machines and you have been asked to design a vehicle for the Chief Scout. We want you to design this vehicle keeping in mind that the Chief Scout would use it for driving around rugged countryside areas, visiting Cub Scout camps and for driving in busy city centres. You can use pencils, paints, crayons, felt-tips, collage . . . in fact anything you want, so long as your picture is no larger than A4 size.

You *must* write your name, age and address on the back of your entry and send it to:

**Micro Machines Competition,
The Cub Scout Annual 1992,
Editorial Department,
The Scout Association,
Baden-Powell House,
Queen's Gate,
LONDON,
SW7 5JS**

RULES
1. **The finished picture must be no larger than A4 (the same size as this page).**
2. **All competitors must be under 11 years old on December 31st, 1992.**
3. **The closing date for entries is January 31st, 1992.**
4. **The Editor's decision is final. No correspondence can be entered into and no entries can be returned unless accompanied by a stamped, self-addressed envelope.**

**Micro Machine
Race in a Case**

CUB SCOUT 'CHUCKLES'

Q. What's green and sings?

A. Elvis Parsley.

Q. What's an ig?
A. An Eskimo's house without a loo.

Q. How many ears did Davy Crockett have?
A. Three – a left ear, a right ear and a wild frontier.

Q. What do you call a snake with a briefcase and a bowler hat?

A. A civil serpent.

Q. Where do baby gorillas sleep?
A. In apricots.

Q. What kind of lights did Noah have on the ark?
A. Floodlights.

Q. What's short, green and goes camping?
A. A Cub Sprout.

Q. If you were surrounded by six elephants, eight horses, six tigers, four lions, six monkeys and two giraffes, how would you get away?
A. Stop the merry-go-round and get off.

Q. What do you call a one-eyed dinosaur?

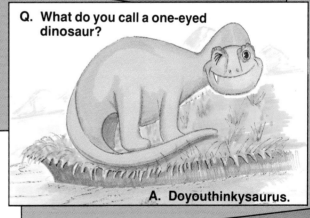

A. Doyouthinkysaurus.

Q. Why is Doctor Frankenstein never lonely?

A. He's good at making friends.

Q. What lies in a cot and wobbles?
A. A jelly baby.

Q. How did the baker get an electric shock?
A. He stepped on a bun and a currant ran up his leg.

A Monster Feast

With a little bit of imagination, a little bit of food colouring and LOTS of mess, you can cook yourself and your friends a fantastic beastly feast, and have a great party with a difference. All of the following recipes are based on a Monster theme, which makes cookery so much more interesting and more fun to eat.

Most adults will probably think the end results are pretty revolting, but who wants to make fairy cakes when with the minimum of effort you can have delicious gory-looking milkshakes, fingers, eyeballs, teeth and lots more brilliant party food ideas that will wow your friends?

The recipes on the following pages are for fun food with a difference so go ahead and throw a Monster party!

Caroline '91

Recipes

Before you start:

Although the following recipes are easy and designed to be lots of fun, some do involve using the oven, so use these simple guidelines to make sure that what you are doing is safe and you don't blow up the kitchen or wreck any of the pots and pans!

Always wash your hands before handling food.

Make sure that you have all the ingredients and utensils to hand, before you start to cook.

Never leave saucepan handles sticking out from the stove and be especially careful when using hot or boiling water.

Always use oven gloves when taking anything out of the oven.

Be really careful when using knives and use a chopping board.

Make sure that you wash up and leave everywhere clean and tidy when you have finished. Clean up as you go along, if possible.

If you are unsure about anything, ask an adult to help you.

Monster Face Pizza

Pizza bases or pitta bread
A mixture of any of the following:
Tomato puree
Slices of cheese (Mozzarella if sliced or Cheddar if grated)
Carrots, cut into strips
Gherkins
Tomatoes (sliced)
Red, yellow or green peppers
Pickled onions
Cucumber
Hard boiled eggs
Sausages
Sliced salami or pepperoni
Bacon strips
Ham
Tinned spaghetti, or other pasta shapes
Mushrooms

The list is endless, simply choose what you fancy, make up your own combinations or use what is available.

Spread tomato puree quite thickly over the pizza bases or pitta bread (don't cut the pitta bread open, just spread the puree on one side).

Add slices of cheese on top of the tomato puree, just enough so that your monster face has a nice cheese and tomato base to it. Put the pizza under the grill for a few minutes until the cheese is bubbling, then take it out and use any combination you like to make a really horrible monster face. A rasher of bacon makes a mouth, a mushroom for a nose, tinned spaghetti hair, salami eyes – the combinations are endless! Cut vegetables into noses or fangs with carrot eyebrows and boiled egg slices for eyes. As soon as your monster looks really gross, pop it back under the grill for another couple of minutes to warm it up again and then eat it!

Crunchy Monster Fingers

Slices of ham
Peanut butter
Cottage cheese
Cucumber, apple or pineapple

Spread the peanut butter fairly thinly on the ham slices, leaving the edges clear. Then spread the cottage cheese on top. Chop up the apple, cucumber or pineapple (all three if you like) and then scatter along one edge of the ham. Next, roll the ham up and the fingers are ready to eat.

You can try combinations of lots of other different fillings for the fingers, but don't be tempted to put too much in or they will become very messy.

Monsters' Eyeballs

Tomatoes (large ones are easier to work with but small ones will do just as well)
Choose from various fillings such as:
Tinned tuna fish (drained)
Parsley (dried or fresh)
OR
Baked beans
Grated cheese
OR
Scrambled egg

Slice the tops off the tomatoes and put to one side. Scoop out the pulp and mix it with the filling of your choice, then refill the tomato. Put the top back on again and heat under a medium grill for about 10 minutes.

Blood Streaked Fingers

Sausages (1 or 2 per person)
A rasher of streaky bacon per sausage
Grated cheese
Pickle
Tomato sauce
Toothpicks

Carefully slit the sausages from end to end using a sharp knife. Open them out and crumble some cheese into the middle of each. Then, if liked, spread a little pickle on top of the cheese. Close the sausages together and wrap a rasher of bacon around each one. Use the toothpicks at each end to hold the fingers with.

Heat under a medium grill for 8–10 minutes or until the bacon is crispy.

Serve covered with blood (tomato sauce)!

Monsters' Teeth

6 oz (150g) popping corn
2 tablespoons vegetable oil
1 apple, cored and finely chopped
1½ cups golden syrup
1 tablespoon white vinegar
1 teaspoon salt
2 teaspoons vanilla essence
(optional)

Popcorn is very easy to make but be sure that you use a saucepan with a tight-fitting lid as the corn literally explodes in the hot oil.

Heat the oil in a large saucepan until it is hot (ask an adult to tell you when it is hot enough). Test it by dropping one piece of corn in. If it starts to pop the oil is ready.

Put the rest of the corn in the pan, put the lid on and listen for the popping. Shake the pan from time to time. After a few minutes the popping should stop.

Give it another few seconds to make sure that all the grains have popped and it is ready.

Core and chop the apple finely, leaving the skin on, and mix well with the popped corn.

Put the syrup, salt and vinegar in another saucepan and bring to the boil. Boil without stirring until it begins to go hard. Remove from the heat and add vanilla essence (or peppermint works well). Pour over the corn and toss until each piece is well coated. Allow to cool a little but ensure that the coating doesn't completely solidify. If it starts to do this, warm it again gently over a low heat. Rub some butter into your hands, to prevent the mixture sticking to your fingers and shape into clusters. Leave to harden properly, then eat.

Monstrous Cake

All parties need a cake to round things off so here's a recipe for a huge, gruesome one!

Make the cake round, square or oblong depending on what type of cake tins you can find or on what you prefer. You can always cut the cake into a different shape once it is cooked, if you like.

4oz (100g) soft butter or margarine
4oz (100g) caster sugar
2 eggs
6oz (150g) self-raising flour
Jam
Margarine for greasing the tins
Greaseproof paper
A packet of icing sugar

To decorate:
Jam, food colouring, chocolate drops, twigs etc, dried fruit, glacé cherries, hundreds and thousands, nuts, jelly sweets, ice cream cones, liquorice, or whatever else you like.

To make a sponge cake:

Preheat the oven to gas mark 4/180C/350F.

Grease the cake tins with a little butter or margarine and line the bottom of each tin with greaseproof paper.

Mix the butter and sugar together in a big mixing bowl using a wooden spoon. Keep mixing until the mixture is fluffy and all the butter and sugar are mixed up well together (if you are not sure if it's mixed properly, ask your mum, she's probably an expert!).

Break the eggs into a smaller bowl and beat them with a fork, then gradually mix them into the butter and sugar mixture, beating them in well.

Sift the flour into yet another bowl (it's a messy business this cake-making)!

Stir half of the sieved flour into the mixture then gradually add the rest. Mix it in well, then pour into the cake tin and place in the oven for 20–25 minutes.

After the cooking time is up, take the tin out using an oven glove and place the cake on a wire rack to cool.

When it is cool, carefully cut it through the middle into two halves and spread jam quite thickly on the bottom half to sandwich the two halves together.

To make the icing, carefully follow the instructions on the packet, which are really simple: icing sugar is just mixed with water. However, be really careful and ask your mum or dad to give you a hand as it is very easy to add too much water and make it really sloppy. If you do want to cut your cake up into a different shape, now is the time to do so. Use the icing as glue.

Let the icing set and then have fun decorating your monstrous cake. It's really good fun having a big gooey cake to cover in sweets so be as inventive as you can and make your cake look really horrible!

There is another recipe on page 61.

CUB SCOUTING WORDSEARCH

Hidden in the wordsquare are 35 things which are connected in some way with Cub Scouting. Many of them are names of Activity Badges, some are names of Jungle animals, some are just things with which any good Cub Scout will be familiar. The words run horizontally, diagonally and vertically, backwards and forwards. To help you along, all the words are listed below.

When you have found them all there will be 22 letters left that have not been used. Read in order, these will give you the name of something which all Cub Scouts should be aiming for.

```
R E V O L L A M I N A T H T B W
E N M A N A T U R A L I S T O G
N T B O D W H S I X V I N R O A
A E P A U E L I H C T A L E K R
I R L C D N E C N R M D S E R D
R T E Y H G T I A Y F I L A E E
O A H C A T E A D R M A M U A N
T I E L T R W N I O P A C K D E
S N M I H R A E R N E K A C E R
I E O S I H N P S W I M M E R S
H R H T R D E R E R O L P X E E
L P E R S O N A L S A F E T Y I
A R S H T N A M S T F A R C A B
C W I R O T A C I N U M M O C B
O P H O T O G R A P H E R A R O
L C O O K D Y T E F A S E M O H
```

AKELA	ENTERTAINER	MUSICIAN
ANIMAL LOVER	EXPLORER	NATURALIST
ARTIST	GARDENER	PACK
ATHLETE	HANDYMAN	PERSONAL SAFETY
BADGE	HATHI	PHOTOGRAPHER
BOOK READER	HOBBIES	PROMISE
CAMPER	HOME HELP	RAMA
CHIL	HOME SAFETY	SIX
COOK	KAA	SWIMMER
COMMUNICATOR	LAW	WORLD FRIENDSHIP
CRAFTSMAN	LOCAL HISTORIAN	WRITER
CYCLIST	MOUNTAIN	

Answer on page 61

JUGGLING

If you have ever been to a circus or watched a variety show on television the chances are you will have seen somebody juggling – that is, continuously tossing into the air, and catching, several objects seemingly all at the same time. Have you ever wished you could do that? Well, you can. Although juggling requires a little bit of practice and a *lot* of patience it really is quite easy if you put your mind to it. The following is a brief and simple guide to the basics of juggling and, given time, should help you on your way to becoming the Juggling King of your Cub Scout Pack.

Firstly, find three objects of similar shape, size and weight with which to juggle. Objects which fit comfortably into your hands are best e.g. bean bags, tennis balls, apples. Bean bags are particularly good because they don't roll away when you drop them and are less likely to damage your parents' priceless pieces of china should you hurl them in the wrong direction. Of course chasing after tennis balls (and running away from your angry parents) does have the advantage of keeping you fit, but that really isn't the object of this exercise.

1. Once you have decided upon your objects (I'll call them balls from now on to make it easier) pick them up, two in one hand and one in the other.

2. Using a smooth scooping motion with your hand, toss one of the balls (from the hand holding two) up into the air. The ball should travel in a smooth arc from one hand to the other.

3. As the first ball reaches the top of the arc, toss the single ball from the other hand in a similar way but just inside the arc made by the first ball.

4. One of your hands should now be free and it is with this hand that you now catch the first ball to be tossed.

5. Remember that at this point the second ball tossed is still in the air travelling in an arc towards the hand from which the first ball came. Before the second ball lands you have to toss the third ball (from the hand which originally held two balls) in that familiar arc, just inside that of the ball which is about to land.

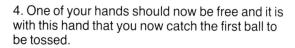

6. You then catch the second ball in the free hand. Meanwhile, the third ball is in the air on its way to your other hand.

7. Now, toss the ball from the hand where the third ball is about to land inside the arc of the already airborne ball and then catch the already airborne ball.

8. And that's it! You're juggling! Simply repeat the above instructions until your arms fall off or until you drop one, or all, of the balls.

BE A CLOWN!

Once your juggling skills are up to performance standard why not show them off to your Pack and put on a show! Dressing up as a clown is simple and effective and would really make you feel the part.

All you need is: **A set of face paints or stage make-up * An old floppy hat**

Some orange or red wool * A big man's jacket

Big buttons or pompons * A bow tie * A pair of braces

A big pair of old men's trousers * Some string or old laces

Men's shoes in a large size or plimsolls

Create your own clown's face by experimenting with different colours. Try a white face with red lips, a red nose (of course!) black or multi-coloured eyes and big bushy black eyebrows.

Use glue to stick the wool inside an old hat as clown's hair or just stick a big silly artificial flower to the brim.

If you can, sew some big colourful buttons or pompons down the front of the jacket or, if not, just sew patches of coloured material or paper all over it and tie ribbons through the button holes.

A bow tie and a pair of braces will also add to the effect but they are not essential.

Try to get hold of a big baggy pair of men's trousers if you can or use an old pair of your own. Again, sew patches of coloured material to them and make sure, if they are really baggy, that you tie them up around your waist with string. Roll up the legs a little, so that you can walk properly!

If you can get hold of some shoes that are lots of sizes too big for you, then they will look like the huge shoes that clowns often wear. Be sure to wear a few pairs of socks though, and be really careful not to trip! Alternatively, just wear some of your own plimsolls and add ribbons, bows or pompons to brighten them up.

Remember, the best thing about dressing up as a clown is that you can have as many variations as you like and the best dressed clowns are the most original ones, so use your imagination and go for it! Try out different colours and ways of wearing jackets and shirts, inside out, upside down, whatever you like – the idea is to make people laugh as much as possible. Beg or borrow what you can and think of ways of making the most of simple old things. All the clothes mentioned can easily be picked up at a jumble sale or 'bring and buy' so be on the lookout. You could start a dressing-up box at your Headquarters if there isn't one already. If there is – ask Akela if you can raid it!

1916 and all that ...

Wolf Cubs circa 1916.

In 1991 the Cub Scout Section celebrated a very special occasion – its 75th anniversary. The Cub Scout Section of the Scout Movement has undergone a great many changes over the years since their humble beginnings as Wolf Cubs, the most obvious being a change of name. Here, Ron Crabb takes a look back at how it all began, how the Section grew and has a quick look at what the future might hold.

'Why can't we join?'

'Why can't we join?' was the question asked by many young boys aged about 8 to 11 years old, as they saw how much fun their older brothers and friends were having at Scouts – it was this question that prompted the beginning of Cub Scouting.

When, in 1908, Baden-Powell wrote *Scouting for Boys* his original intention was that Scouting should be for boys between the ages of 11 and 18. In a short period of time Scouting began to spread across the country so fast that boys who had begun to practise what B.-P. had written in his book needed adult leaders to help them to do it properly – this was the birth of the first Scout Troops.

Often, younger boys would hurry along to their nearest Scout Troop and ask if they could join, usually only to be turned away, but some boys would not take no for an answer and bothered the Scoutmasters (now called Scout Leaders) so many times that in the end they decided to let these younger boys join in.

The boys were formed into their own 'Scout Cadet Corps' and because they had no rules or uniform as such, they invented them. Their uniform was loosely based upon the Scout uniform; they wore a wide brimmed hat like the Scouts but instead of a proper Scout stave, they would use a broom handle which was nearer to their size!

What will we call them?

B.-P. could see how boys would benefit from being 'Junior Scouts', as he first called them, and he immediately set to work on creating activities and a book for this new Section of the Scout Movement, but more important than this was to think of a name for these keen boys.

He realised immediately that he had already written in *Scouting for Boys* about the way in which Red Indians would describe good scouts as being 'wolves'. Using this idea B.-P. decided upon a name for the young boys who were learning to be 'wolves'. That name was 'Wolf Cubs'.

Baden-Powell knew that the ideas behind the Wolf Cubs had to be full of fun and excitement and that they had to provide the boys in that age range with something completely different from anything else. He thought that if this new Section of the Movement was going to be called the Wolf Cubs then, perhaps, it should be based upon a tale of real wolves in a jungle, which was where one of Baden-Powell's good friends, Rudyard Kipling, came into the story.

Rudyard Kipling had written a book called *The Jungle Book*, which told stories of adventure and courage in the jungle, all of which were ideas that appealed to Baden-Powell. So, in 1916, *The Wolf Cub's Handbook* was published, all of the questions about what to do with the Junior Scouts were answered and the Wolf Cub idea was so popular that the handbook sold out in the shops almost immediately.

On June 24, 1916, the first Conference of Cubmasters met at the Headquarters of the then Boy Scouts Association (now called The Scout Association) to discuss the future of the Wolf Cub Section. The conference was attended by Baden-Powell, the Chief Scout, and Lady Baden-Powell, along with some 80 Leaders, who reported that at that time there were approximately 6,000 to 8,000 boys in the Junior Scouts already.

It's official!

On December 16, 1916, in London's Caxton Hall, a large audience attended the first public demonstration of the Wolf Cubs as the junior branch of the Boy Scout Movement, and the public liked what they saw!

The Wolf Cub uniform was made up of a green jersey, a yellow neckerchief which was knotted near the throat, and a green cap with yellow piping which had the Wolf Cub Badge on the front. Some boys would tie the loose ends of their scarf with a thumb knot which Baden-Powell said should remind them to do their Good Turn. The complete uniform for a Wolf Cub would have cost ten shillings, the equivalent of 50 pence today.

A new Wolf Cub was called a 'Tenderpad' because, just like a real wolf cub beginning his life of adventure, he would suffer from sore feet or make a few mistakes until he had learnt a few dodges.

A group of Wolf Cubs was called a Pack, and remains so today. Many Packs had totem poles featuring a wolf's head on the top, which they would carry with them wherever they went.

Instead of the Scout Sign and Salute being made with three fingers, when Wolf Cubs first started only two fingers were used, representing the two ears of the wolf.

During their time in the Wolf Cubs, boys had the opportunity to work towards many badges. The first two were called the First and Second Stars and for these one had to be able to do a number of activities, such as be able to somersault, balance on a narrow plank of wood, as well as know about the country's flag, the National Anthem, knots, compass work, fire lighting and first aid.

If you were a Wolf Cub in those days you would have been given nine months in which to finish your Second Star, then both of your Stars would be sewn onto the front of your cap, so that they looked as if they were a wolf's eyes.

Members of the 16th North Poplar (Bow Church) Wolf Cub Pack, who took part in the first Wolf Cub demonstration at Caxton Hall, London, on December 16th, 1916.

Baden-Powell with Cubs and Scouts of the South African contingent at the World Jamboree 1929, held at Arrowe Park, Birkenhead.

Next, boys could work towards gaining some of the 12 Proficiency Badges which were very popular, with titles such as the Collector and the Team Player.

Instead of the Seconds' and Sixers' badges which exist today, a Second, Sixer or even Senior Sixer could be recognised by counting the one, two or three large yellow stripes which were worn on the left arm.

The last badge which a Wolf Cub would complete was the Leaping Wolf Badge, which acted as a link between the Wolf Cub Pack and the Scout Troop, but this badge was not introduced until some years later.

When the first official census was taken in September 1917, the membership figures had risen to 28,450 in Britain alone and many more Wolf Cubs were starting up in other countries.

Three years later, in 1920, London hosted the first World Jamboree attended by Scouts from all over the world. The Wolf Cubs had become a well supported Section of the Movement and put on displays of games and activities showing everybody the sort of things that Wolf Cubs do. It was definitely evident that the Wolf Cubs were living up to their Wolf Cub Motto – 'Do your best'.

Cub Scout outdoor handicrafts at Gilwell Park, 1987.

The wolf was no more!

Over the years the activities which Wolf Cubs took part in began to develop and more Proficiency Badges became available. In 1967, as a result of a special report commissioned by the Chief Scout at that time, Sir Charles Maclean (who later became Lord Maclean), many changes were made, the most important one being to change the name of the Section to Cub Scouts.

Cubmasters became known as Cub Scout Leaders and the idea of the progressive Star Badges was replaced by the Arrow Award Scheme, which has in turn recently been replaced by the Cub Scout Award, Adventure Award, Adventure Crest Award and Cub Scout Challenge.

Another major change was the re-wording of the Cub Scout Law from what it used to read:

1. The Cub gives in to the old Wolf.

2. The Cub does not give in to himself.

to the Cub Scout Law which we use today.

Cub Scouting goes into the 90s. A new training programme and new members.

Cub Scouts reach across the world

Over the years 'Cub Scout' has become a household name, with Cubs becoming well known for aiming to 'do their best' and their willingness to help other people. It is often as a result of a Cub Scout helping somebody that the Section's (and the Movement's) reputation has spread, often with that person showing an interest in helping the Movement by becoming a Leader.

Other countries have seen the benefits of having Cub Scouts in their country and they have been granted permission to join the World Scout Association.

Girls in the Cub Scout Pack?

In the same way that those original 8 to 11 year old boys had been plaguing the Scoutmasters to let them join, in the few years leading up to 1990 many girls had been asking if they could join the Cub Scout and Scout Sections of the Movement.

So, in 1990 the long decision-making process of whether or not girls should be allowed to join the younger Sections of The Scout Association began. Obviously a lot of different things would have to be considered, much in the same way that Baden-Powell had tackled the question of what to do with the boys who wanted to know 'Why can't we join?'

Into the future

As long as there are people who are willing to be Leaders, there is no reason at all why Cub Scouting will ever fade away. The 1990 census showed that there were 243,807 Cub Scouts in Britain and that there is the potential for many more as the Cub Scout Section passed through its 75th anniversary year in 1991.

1991 also saw the beginning of a brand new training programme for Cub Scouts offering more challenge and adventure than ever before.

Baden-Powell managed to create the greatest youth organisation ever, an organisation in which Cub Scouting plays an enormous part. As part of a rapidly progressing Movement, nobody can predict what the future may hold for Cub Scouting, but there is one thing of which we can all be sure – it's certainly going to be bright!

Fabulous Beasts & Incredible Creatures

ABOMINABLE SNOWMAN

Also known as 'Bigfoot' or 'Yeti' the Abominable Snowman is believed to be a large, hairy manlike creature from the Himalayas. Reports of the existence of such a creature have been current since 1832. These reports gained a significant amount of substance in 1951 when Eric Shipton of the Everest Reconnaissance Expedition produced a photograph of a large footprint in the snow said to have been that of the Abominable Snowman.

VAMPIRES

One of the most famous types of all monsters, vampires originated from the demonology of the Slavonic peoples, who believed that vampires were ghosts or spirits who rose from the grave at night to suck the blood of sleeping men. Not all vampires' victims died, but those who did became vampires themselves. Vampires were said to have the ability to turn into bats, wolves or even smoke. There are a lot of different opinions about the best way of destroying vampires but the most popular are sunlight and a wooden stake driven through the monster's heart.

WEREWOLVES

'Even a man who is pure of heart and says his prayers at night,
Can become a wolf when the wolfbane blooms and the moon is full and bright.'
Or so the poem goes. Werewolves, or wolfmen, are mortal men who turn into wolves whenever there is a full moon. This condition was believed to be caused by being bitten (but not killed by) another werewolf. The best way to kill a werewolf is to shoot him (or her) with a silver bullet, preferably fired by somebody who loves the werewolf in his or her human form.

CLIFF BROWN'S PUZZLE PAGE

Wildlife Acrostic
Here is a puzzle for holders of the Naturalist and World Conservation Activity Badges.

First identify the creatures pictured; they are your 'across' clues.
Put them in the correct order in the grid and the name of another animal will appear in the diagonal circles.

Check your answer on page 61.

FUDGING THE TRUTH

There were only two things wrong with Elvis Tobin. One of those things was his name. You see, Elvis' dad was, unfortunately, a big fan of Elvis Presley, the rock and roll singer. So much so that he had decided to name his only son after the King of Rock and Roll. It was not much fun being a nine-year-old called Elvis. Of course, it could have been worse. His dad could have been a Kylie Minogue fan.

However, the other bad thing about Elvis Tobin was that he simply could not resist the urge to tell fibs, both large and small, but usually large. In fact, he loved to tell whoppers, the kind of lies so great they were simply absurd and totally unbelievable. If Elvis Presley was the King of Rock and Roll, then Elvis Tobin was the King of the Liars. For this reason, nobody much believed anything that Elvis told them and nobody ever really took him seriously. If anything, his lies were quite amusing and good for a laugh.

There were many good things about Elvis, too, and one was that he was a Cub Scout and attended Cub Scouts regularly every Thursday night. One night, shortly before the Grand Howl, he was chatting with two of his friends, Philip and Kevin.

'My dad has just bought a satellite dish for our television,' Kevin proudly told his friends, 'so now we can get eight different channels. It's brilliant. As well as the usual channels we can get the Movie Channel, the Disney Channel, the Sports Channel and MTV. You

can come around to my house and watch them if you like.'

'That's nothing,' said Elvis. 'Our TV has fifty-four different channels. We can get programmes from America, Italy, Sweden . . . anywhere.'

'Excellent!' said Philip. 'Can we come and watch yours instead?'

'Er, I'm not sure my dad will let you. He likes to play his records a lot and he's not too keen on people coming around to watch the telly,' replied Elvis. Of course, Elvis' friends knew what this meant although they didn't mind too much.

'Pack, Pack, Pack,' called Akela, and the meeting began. It was a particularly important meeting that night because the Pack were finalising the details for their Fund Raising Gala which was to take place on Saturday in the field next to the Scout Hall. All the Members were to be given various duties to take care of on the day. The meeting went well and the three friends were happy with their appointed tasks. Kevin and another Cub Scout would be running the coconut shy, Philip was going to sell raffle tickets and Elvis would be selling chocolate fudge cakes which the Pack were going to bake on Saturday morning.

The next day after school, the three friends ended up at Kevin's house watching the Movie Channel whilst sharing an enormous barrel of popcorn and a huge bottle of lemonade. The film they were watching was about some astronauts who had accidentally landed on a strange planet inhabited by a race of aliens, called Sararians, who killed people by pulling faces at them. The faces they pulled were so grotesque that the humans instantly collapsed in a heap, at which point they were promptly eaten by the ugly extra-terrestrials. The film featured a vast array of weapons with which the humans tried to destroy the aliens.

'Those guns are pretty cool, aren't they?' said Philip, admiring a particularly nasty looking weapon which had just been used to turn one of the aliens into something similar to an exploding box of red confetti.

'Yeah,' answered Kevin. 'It's a good thing they aren't real though. Guns that people have nowadays are bad enough. I don't think people should be allowed to use guns at all, not even for hunting.'

'Those guns are copies of a real one. My uncle who used to be a Marine has got one. It's top secret and he's got the only one in the world. He uses it when he goes fishing because, he says, it's better than sitting around all day with a fishing rod.' No prizes for guessing who made this comment, but again the other two didn't really take much notice. They had expected Elvis to come up with a much bigger lie than that.

After the film, Elvis had to go home.

'My dad told me to get back,' he told his friends. 'It's Karaoke night at the community centre and Dad likes me to help him to get ready. Maybe he'll let me go with him tonight,' Elvis added half to himself as he went out of the door, 'I've got a natural gift for music, I can read it blindfolded . . .'

Philip had decided to stay at Kevin's for a little while longer before going home himself.

'Do you think Elvis will ever stop telling lies?' Philip asked Kevin.

'I don't know,' replied Kevin. 'They are funny though, aren't they? Do you remember when he said he'd seen a shark in the river and the Boat Club had to cancel their Annual Canoe Race? That was funny.'

'Yes, but he could get himself into big trouble. What about that time he was late for school and, when Mrs Fielding asked him why, he said that a lion had escaped from the zoo and found its way into his back garden. He said he had to help the people from the zoo to catch the lion and return it to its cage. It was really funny but he got three days' detention for that.'

'Only because Mrs Fielding telephoned the zoo to check the story and found out that he'd been lying.'

'Well, I think it's time he stopped. Maybe we should tell him.'

The next day was Saturday, the day of the Gala. The Gala itself didn't officially begin until 2.00 pm (it was being opened by a local celebrity known only as 'El Mystico – Mind Reader, Memory Man and Magician Extraordinaire') but the Cub Scouts had to be at the Scout Hut by 10.00 am in order to bake the fudge cakes for Elvis' stall and to get things ready generally.

Everybody arrived on time and the Scout Hall and surrounding field were soon buzzing with busy Cub Scouts. The day had started out cloudy but as the morning flew by, the dull weather gave way to blazing sunshine and by 1.45 pm everything was ready for what promised to be a most successful event. It seemed like half the population of the town was already queueing to get in.

At 2.00 pm precisely, El Mystico and his assistant, Sharon arrived at the entrance to the field as the local Scout band struck up a great fanfare. Strung between the gateposts was a thick, silken, red ribbon. Sharon had an enormous pair of scissors which she handed to El Mystico. Taking the scissors, he thanked her and began the day's proceedings.

'It is with great pleasure that I declare the Cub Scouts' Fund Raising Gala open . . . sesame!' With that there was a flash, a bang and a great deal of smoke into which disappeared the magician, his assistant, the scissors, the red ribbon *and* one of the gateposts. It was a most impressive start to a great day. Incidentally, El Mystico and Sharon reappeared later on in the afternoon and performed some more startling tricks, but the gatepost was never seen again!

Philip, Kevin and Elvis watched the opening ceremony from their respective stalls situated in the field. Both Philip and Kevin were amazed at this stunt but Elvis was unimpressed.

'That's nothing,' he shouted to his friends. 'Once, when I was in London, I saw a magician make Nelson's Column disappear.' The other two gave each other a knowing grin.

The good weather had obviously brought out the

crowds. All day long people queued to get into the Gala and, once inside, they kept all the Cub Scouts who were running the stalls very busy indeed. That is, all the Cubs except for Elvis. You see, the weather was so warm that nobody felt much like eating cake. Everybody wanted soft drinks and ice cream. Halfway through the afternoon Akela decided to stroll around to see how the Cubs were getting on.

'Hello, Kevin. How are you and David doing?' she asked the boys at the coconut shy.

'Brilliant!' they answered in unison.

'Yeah, we've had about two hundred and fifty customers so far,' added Kevin.

At Philip's raffle ticket stall Akela received a similar response.

'I've sold five hundred tickets already,' he eagerly announced. Akela continued her way around the site and eventually ended up at the cake stall.

'Hello, Elvis. How's business? The others are doing really well. Kevin's had two hundred and fifty customers and Philip's sold five hundred raffle tickets. Are the cakes selling? I haven't seen many people eating them.'

'That's because the people are eating them so fast. I've already sold about three hundred,' he lied, not wishing to be outdone by his friends' success. In reality he had sold forty-three cakes but Akela couldn't tell how many Elvis still had left because he was keeping them well hidden in a fridge at the back of the stall.

'Well, keep up the good work,' said Akela as she left. It suddenly dawned on Elvis that he would have to get rid of an awful lot of cakes in a hurry.

During one of the many quiet periods at the cake stall, Elvis noticed a dog sniffing around at the back of the tent which served as the temporary cake shop. This gave him an idea.

'Here, doggy,' said Elvis, tossing a cake towards the dog. The hound leapt and caught the cake in mid-air, practically finishing it before landing. On seeing this Elvis decided to give one cake to the dog for every cake sold.

As the afternoon wore on, with the sun setting, the temperature began to drop and sales of cakes began to rise. Elvis was still giving the dog cakes and on his third trip to the back of the tent to give the dog its fifteenth cake, Elvis saw that the dog had now been joined by two others. So, for each cake sold, each dog was given a cake. Half an hour later there were four more dogs at the back of the tent. An hour later an additional five had shown up. By the time the Gala ended there were twenty satisfied dogs at the back of the cake stall, there was one satisifed Cub Scout at the front and there were five cakes left unsold. Unfortunately, Elvis had forgotten something.

After everything had been packed away Akela gathered the Cubs together to see how everything had gone. It had been a very successful event and all the Cubs were pleased with their performances.

'I sold out of all my cakes except for five,' boasted Elvis, still forgetting one important thing.

'Right,' said Akela, 'let's get all our takings collected and we'll put the money into the bank. Let me see now. Elvis, you had five hundred cakes at twenty pence each and you sold four hundred and ninety-five. That's ninety-nine pounds. Well done.'

Suddenly, Elvis wished he were somewhere else – anywhere else. Ninety-nine pounds! Where on earth was he going to get ninety-nine pounds? He had, in actual fact, only sold one hundred and twenty cakes and therefore only had twenty-four pounds. His brain immediately switched over to automatic pilot and he did the only thing he could think of.

'Erm, some bullies came and stole most of the cakes. I had to throw a lot of the cakes away because they went stale in the heat. El Mystico accidentally made them disappear when one his tricks went wrong . . .' Elvis gave the performance of his life. Without pausing for breath he told twenty-one different lies about what had happened to the cakes.

'Elvis,' said Akela, 'things will be a lot easier if you just tell the truth.' Embarrassed, Elvis gave Akela the full story about the dogs and how he was only trying to be as successful as his friends.

'It doesn't matter how well other people are doing. As long as you do your best then that's good enough. We are all working for the same cause here and it's not a competition,' said Akela. 'And it's not so bad that you didn't sell all of your cakes. What is bad is the fact that you lied about it. Lying is a terrible thing. It's not big, it's not funny and it's not clever. I think you owe it to your friends here to try and make up the missing money and I want you to promise that you won't tell any more lies.'

Elvis spent the next four Saturdays washing cars in order to raise the funds lost by his feeding the dogs of the town. Of course, his friends Philip and Kevin volunteered to help him and the three boys managed to double the funds made on the day of the Gala. Elvis had learnt his lesson and even to this day has never, ever told a lie. Honest!

CUB SCOUT 'CHUCKLES'

Q. Which pop group kills all known germs?
A. The Bleach Boys.

Q. What do zombies put on their roast dinner?
A. Grave-y.

Q. What is a sea monster's favourite meal?
A. Fish and ships.

Q. What do you call a cat from the Wild West?

A. A posse cat.

Q. What do you call a collection of skunks?

A. A phew.

Q. What do you get if you pull your knickers up to your armpits?
A. A chest of drawers.

Q. What do ghouls have for dinner?
A. Goulash.

Q. Why was the ghost thrown out of the wine bar?
A. Because they don't serve spirits after 11 pm.

Q. What do you call two spiders who have just been married?

A. Newly webs.

Q. What television programme does Jaws like to watch?

A. Name That Tuna.

If it Moves, Shoot it!

If it doesn't move, shoot it anyway! Don't worry, this is not a feature on guns, it's all about shooting pictures. Indirectly, photography affects almost everybody in some way on a fairly regular basis. Think of how many photographs each person sees every day in newspapers, magazines, books and leaflets; on posters and advertisements; on television; on packaging, etc. After speech and the written word, photography is one of the world's most important means of communication. Apart from that, it's also a great hobby.

Obviously, with such a vast subject it would be impossible to cover all aspects of it here, and anyone looking for more detailed information will be able to find it in one of the countless books written about photography. The aim of this feature is to try to cover the requirements of the Cub Scout Photographer Activity Badge and, hopefully, inspire any budding David Baileys (who's he?) to find out more about photography and to develop their skills.

The principle of photography is simple. The word itself comes from the Greek 'photos', meaning 'light', and 'graphos' meaning 'writing' – writing with light! When a photograph is taken light is directed, usually via a lens, onto light-sensitive film, where an image is produced. At this stage the image is in grades of shadow or negative. The film is then processed and developed to produce a positive printed image.

There are lots of different types of camera available and they come in all shapes and sizes. The most popular types are those that use either 35mm or 110mm (cassette) film and, of course, the instant film cameras, which are great for taking pictures at parties or on occasions when you can't wait to see the picture! Whichever camera you use, the best way to familiarise yourself with its operational features is to read the operating manual or instruction booklet supplied with it.

Although most cameras can produce fairly good pictures when used under the right conditions, those who are serious about taking up photography as a hobby, or even a career, should invest in a good quality 35mm single reflex camera (SLR) similar to the one shown in the diagram. It is this type of camera that we will be dealing with here as it allows the user manual control over focus, shutter speed, depth of field, etc, and the ability to interchange lenses.

Focus

Some cameras have automatic focusing but it is better to use a camera which has focus control. This allows the photographer to focus precisely on the subject within a certain distance range. The focus control (or ring) is located on the lens and rotates for focusing. The way to focus is to view the image carefully through the viewfinder and adjust the lens until the image (or the subject) is sharp and not blurred or fuzzy.

Aperture and Shutter

When a photograph is taken light enters the camera through the lens and exposes the film when the shutter is opened. The lens has an iris much like the human eye, but consisting of a system of metal leaves which open and close. The space in the middle is the aperture, the size of which is measured in f/stops – the smaller the f/stop the wider the opening. The amount of light entering and hitting the film is controlled by both the shutter speed and the aperture setting. Like the focus control the aperture control is located on the lens and is operated by a rotating ring. The aperture governs the volume of light landing on the film and the

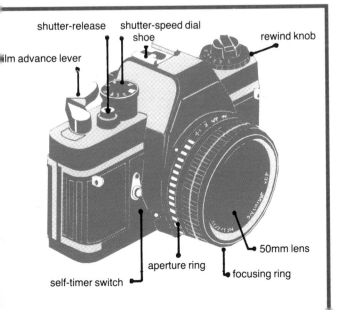

shutter-release   shutter-speed dial   shoe   rewind knob
film advance lever
self-timer switch   aperture ring   focusing ring   50mm lens

shutter speed controls the length of time that light is allowed to land on the film. The shutter speed is measured in fractions of a second, eg 1/30, 1/60, 1/500, 1/1000. If the shutter speed is doubled the amount of light is halved. Similarly, this is the effect if the aperture is decreased by one f/stop.

Aperture also determines the depth of field, ie how sharp the picture is in front of and behind the point on which the lens is focused. The smaller the aperture the greater the depth of field. With a large aperture only the very point of focus will be sharp. A scale on the lens indicates the area in focus at each aperture setting.

A relatively slow shutter speed slightly blurs the fast-moving train, giving the impression of movement.

The shutter speed controls the effect of movement by the subject. A fast shutter speed (1/1000) will freeze even the fastest moving object whilst a slow shutter speed (1/30) will slightly blurr a moving object, thereby giving a visual impression of movement.

Film

As well as there being lots of different types of cameras on the market there are also many different types of film manufactured by a number of companies. Photographic films are given a numerical rating which

A zoom lens with the aperture set at f/2.8 was used for this shot. Notice how this affects the depth of field, leaving the background out of focus.

This picture was taken on 100 ISO film, which is ideally suited to shooting in good sunlight.

A shutter speed of 1/1000 of a second was used to 'freeze' the fountains of water.

400 ISO film is particularly good for indoor and low light situations. For this picture, taken at a rock concert, the photographer has relied solely upon the stage lighting rather than using a flash.

indicates the speed of their reaction to light – the higher the number, the faster the film. Two ratings systems are used: the ASA (devised by the American Standards Association) and the ISO (devised by the International Standards Organisation). The latter is gradually replacing the former and, fortunately, both use identical number scales, so 400 ASA film has the same value as 400 ISO film. In terms of performance, a general rule is that 100 ISO film is good for outdoor photography whilst 400 ISO is better for low light situations or for shooting high speed action (eg sports photography).

The Good, the Bad and the Ugly . . .

To be a good photographer one needs to be able to tell the difference between good and bad pictures. Apart from getting the technical bits right (taking the lens cap off and focusing) a photographer should also know how to compose a picture. This involves selecting the best angle from which to shoot and deciding on what to put into a picture and what to leave out. Some of the classic mistakes which every photographer will make at some time are:

– **head or feet of subject cut off**
– **over or under exposure**
– **bad positioning of subject**
– **blurred photographs**

All are easily remedied but, as with most things, it is much easier to learn by making the mistake. When first starting out as a photographer it is very useful to carry a notebook when taking pictures and to keep a record of the camera settings used to obtain a particular shot. Then if something does go wrong the photographer is already half way to finding out why.

What Shall I Shoot?

A good way of developing one's photographic skills is to choose one theme or subject and to take a selection of photographs around that theme or subject. Scouting provides an abundant amount of photographic opportunities and there are many themes which a Cub Scout could choose – a camp or Pack day out, a

Try to avoid shooting directly towards the sun – an interesting effect but not a very good picture.

With the sun behind the camera the result is much more satisfying.

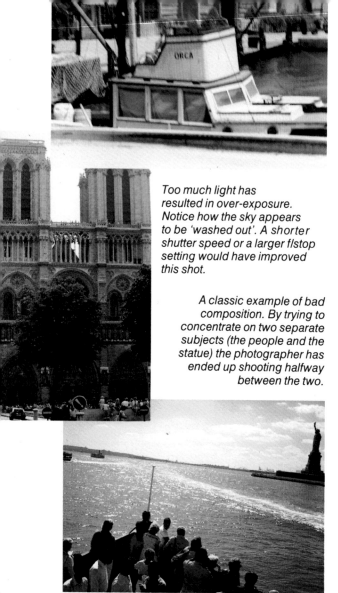

Too much light has resulted in over-exposure. Notice how the sky appears to be 'washed out'. A shorter shutter speed or a larger f/stop setting would have improved this shot.

A classic example of bad composition. By trying to concentrate on two separate subjects (the people and the statue) the photographer has ended up shooting halfway between the two.

A slow shutter speed (1/30 of a second) and an unsteady hand has blurred this photograph. The picture is also very badly composed.

photographic record of a Pack conservation project from start to finish, a study of a local area, nature or wildlife, Pack activities, travel, transport – the list is endless!

Most photographers choose a subject in which they are already interested and concentrate on that particular subject. If the photographer cares about the subject then, as unlikely as it may seem, his or her photographic skills will improve much more quickly simply because people tend to be good at things they enjoy. Most of the world's greatest photographers specialise in one particular subject, eg Lord Lichfield (portraits), Eamonn McCabe (sport), Heather Angel and Stephen Dalton (nature and wildlife). Apart from being among the finest in their own fields they are also excellent all-round photographers.

And Then . . .

One of the requirements of the Cub Scout Photographer Activity Badge is to present a display of photographs (or give a film/video show). Part of the joy of photography is being able to share your results with others. Displaying your pictures is also a great way of finding out what other people think of your pictures. Care should be taken in choosing the pictures to be displayed and in choosing the way in which they are to be displayed. One should always remember that not only is a picture worth a thousand words but also that one *good* picture is worth a thousand bad ones.

If you do decide to take photographs on a 'Cub Scouting' theme, remember that SCOUTING Magazine is always on the lookout for good photographs in its photo competitions, which feature fairly regularly. Ask your Cub Scout Leader to let you know when the next competition is being held. Who knows, your picture could end up on the cover of the Movement's magazine!

Fabulous Beasts & Incredible Creatures

PEGASUS

In Greek mythology, Pegasus was a beautiful winged horse which sprang from the blood of Medusa the gorgon. Ironically, Pegasus became the horse of Perseus, the man who eventually killed Medusa. Pegasus was transformed into a constellation and may often be seen shining brightly in the night sky.

PHOENIX

A miraculous Egyptian bird which, according to legend, burnt itself to death on an altar of aromatic woods after living for 500 years in the Arabian desert. The phoenix then rose from the ashes with its youth restored.

SPHINX

A fabulous monster featured in Egyptian art and represented as a lion with the head of a man. The Great Sphinx at Gizeh in Egypt, a giant statue of the creature, is one of the Seven Wonders of the World. It is 58 metres (189 feet) long and is believed to have been built around 2900 B.C.

UNICORN

Said to have lived in India, the unicorn was a beautiful white horse with one straight horn growing from its forehead. The unicorn was able to outwit anybody who tried to capture it except for pure and innocent youths.

Some of the monsters and creatures mentioned are featured in a great many films (most of which are available on video). Below is a short list of the ones which are fun rather than scary!

Clash of the Titans – Pegasus and Medusa the Gorgon among others
Legend – unicorn
The Lost Boys – vampires
The Monster Squad – vampires, werewolves and others
Silver Bullet – werewolves
Bigfoot and the Hendersons – abominable snowman
The Cyclops – guess what this one is about!
Teen Wolf – werewolves

SPACE EXPLORERS

Pt. 2 the Pedestrian CODE

ART: Steve Harman.

LEGO® ⋺LACKTRON™

Competition

25 LEGO Blacktron Intruder Starships to be won!

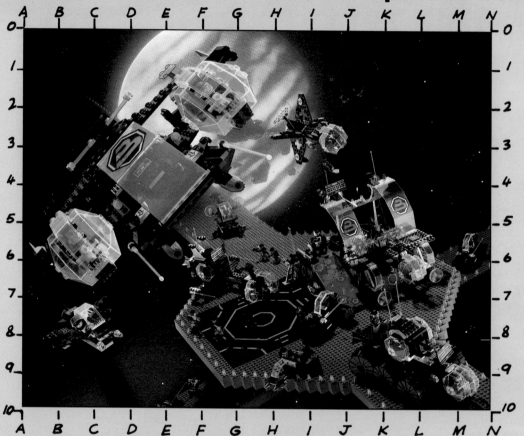

In the picture above, showing all the terrific new LEGO Blacktron range, there is a deliberate mistake – a 'ghost' brick shown in outline only. Simply identify the position of the 'ghost' brick and you could win one of 25 Blacktron Intruder Starship kits (that's the big one in the picture).

How to enter

All you have to do is study the picture carefully and find the 'ghost' brick. Then, use the letters and numbers at the edge of the picture to determine the map reference of the brick, eg 1A.

Write the map reference, together with your name, age and address on a postcard (or the back of a sealed envelope) and send it to the following address to arrive no later than January 31st 1992.

LEGO Blacktron Competition,
The 1992 Cub Scout Annual,
The Publications Department,
The Scout Association,
Baden-Powell House,
Queen's Gate,
LONDON
SW7 5JS

Rules

1. **All competitors must be under 11 years old on December 31st 1992.**
2. **The closing date for entries is January 31st 1992.**
3. **The winners will be the first 25 correct entries picked randomly from all those correct entries received by January 31st 1992.**
4. **The Editor's decision is final. No correspondence will be entered into.**

Zack and the Time Machine

Zack Taylor grinned from ear to ear as he flew around a corner in his home, nearly skidded into a huge suit of armour, and headed for the telephone. Hopping from one foot to the other, Zack dialled his best friend, TJ (short for Tracey-Jane, which she hated), and waited impatiently for her to answer. On the sixth ring, TJ's mum answered and asked Zack to wait. Hardly able to contain himself, Zack continued to hop from side to side and then at last TJ herself came on the line.

'Quick, TJ, can you come around here now?' said Zack. 'I've got something fantastic to show you, only it has to be in the next hour while the builders are at lunch. Ask your mum if you can spend the afternoon here.'

'Wow, slow down, Zack,' said TJ. 'What builders, the ones who are fixing up a studio for your dad in the cellar, you mean? Have they found a skeleton or some treasure down there?'

'No, no, TJ, something better,' said Zack. 'Just come around, okay?'

'Okay, Zack,' said TJ, 'but I was working on the history project. There's only another week left until it has to be in. You have remembered, haven't you?'

'Oh, yeah, I was going to get around to that later.' Zack grinned again. 'I thought you might help me.'

'Look, I'll come round and bring that really great book my mum got for me. You know, the one I was telling you about, with castles in it.'

Ten minutes later, TJ was heading down the hill into Little-Castleton village on her bike. She thought about the mysterious phone call from Zack and wondered what on earth he could be up to this time. She had made friends with Zack when he joined her class at the local school about a month before, in the middle of term. Everyone else had been a bit wary of the new boy, but TJ had made him welcome and they had soon become firm friends.

Zack and his family had moved into the castle at the edge of the village and had been the subject of much gossip as Zack's dad was quite a famous painter and photographer. Their arrival had been doubly interesting for the village as the castle had always belonged to old Mr Taylor (Zack's great uncle), an eccentric old inventor and a real character, who had also made some pretty famous inventions in his day. He was quite gruff but friendly really – and he always let the village fête be held in the castle grounds each year and gave lots of money to the church funds and school fund-raising events. Anyhow, when old Mr Taylor asked Zack's mum and dad if the family would like to come and live with him, sort of indefinitely, to help look after the place, they agreed that it would be a good idea to spend some time in the countryside, so they moved to the castle.

It was quite a small castle as castles go, but it had a moat and a drawbridge, although there was no water in the moat anymore, just grass and flowers and a few geese. Anyhow, TJ thought the castle was great and she was glad that she and Zack were friends as they had such a great time together exploring the place.

When TJ arrived at the castle, she jumped off her bike and headed in across the drawbridge towards the huge front porch. Zack was sitting on the steps waiting for her, fiddling with an old polaroid camera, which was always on the blink. Zack was like his uncle in that he loved gadgets but always fiddled with them to see how they worked and ended up unable to put them back together again.

Zack threw the camera strap over his shoulder when he saw her coming and waved madly. 'Quick, TJ, we don't have much time, the builders will be back from lunch soon and I've got something amazing to show you,' he said. Puzzled, TJ followed Zack through the huge hall of the castle and around to the corridor that led to the kitchens and beyond them the cellars.

Hurrying down the steps, Zack and TJ stopped at the bottom and gazed around. The cellars of the castle were huge, like lots and lots of large rooms leading into each other, and there was quite a lot of old junk around and racks and racks of musty old bottles of wine stacked against the walls.

They moved farther into the cellars, to where the workmen had started to build a photographic studio for Zack's dad, complete with a darkroom for developing pictures. TJ could see ahead to where they had knocked down a wall to make one of the cellar rooms bigger and beyond that, set against the wall, was a door.

'Look at that,' said Zack proudly. 'A secret passage – and there's a corridor behind it. We must find out where it leads.'

'Ace!' said TJ excitedly. 'Let's explore.'

'Okay,' said Zack, and grabbing a torch from the workmen's tools, he moved forward.

Zack and TJ opened the door and shone the torch into the thick blackness beyond. All they could see was the stone floor and walls of a round tunnel-shaped corridor leading upwards. As they started to move along the tunnel they felt the floor beneath them curving up and then down, up and then down, until they were completely disorientated and lost.

'Do you have any idea where this may lead, Zack?' TJ whispered as they trudged along.

'No,' Zack called back, just as the corridor suddenly came to a halt in front of a thick black door.

'TJ, are you okay?' Zack muttered, rubbing his head and looking at the door he had just bumped into.

'Yeah, I'm okay,' answered TJ, looking around. 'This is a pretty cool secret passage you've got here, Zack. C'mon, let's carry on.'

Together they moved forward and tried the door. It took some pushing and shoving but the old door eventually swung open to reveal a musty, oval-shaped room.

'This room must be directly underneath one of the turrets,' Zack exclaimed, shining the torch into the room.

The two kids looked around at what appeared to be a strange kind of workshop. There were benches with old wires and metal objects on them and lots of springs and coils of wire and nuts and bolts all over the floor. Over on the far side of the room loomed a large object covered in a dustcloth. Zack cautiously shone the torch over it and then pulled back the cloth. What was revealed looked a bit like a dodgem car with a sort of radar dish at the top of the wire that usually attaches dodgem cars to the power at a fairground.

'Wow, that looks like a mini-hovercraft to me!' TJ stared at the dodgem car in astonishment.

'Let's check it out.' Zack climbed into the little car and began to push buttons and click switches and turn the little steering wheel. As TJ began to climb into the seat next to Zack, the car began to throb and whir and lights flashed on and off, until suddenly, TJ was thrown backwards into the seat next to Zack as the dodgem car lifted off the ground and began to spin around in a circle, faster and faster and faster.

For a few minutes Zack and TJ were helpless as the car spun them around in a whirl of flashing lights and weird sounds. Then gradually the twirling dodgem car began to slow down, and finally hit the floor again with a jolting bump.

Feeling dizzy and even more disorientated, Zack and TJ sat up in the dodgem car, then both gasped at the scene before them and shrank back down into the seats.

'Uh, TJ, something is wrong,' Zack eventually managed to whisper. 'These people look really weird.'

'Zack, I think we must have gone back in time somehow,' TJ whispered back.

They were looking out from a high balcony into a huge hall which had an enormous fire with three or four cauldrons boiling away on it and big dogs lying in front

of the flames. There were lots of people dashing across the vast stone floor carrying steaming dishes to a huge table near the fire, where it looked as if there was a party going on.

Suddenly there was a shout from below and all the activity in the great hall stopped as everyone gazed upwards at Zack and TJ.

'Look there!' yelled a boy dressed in brightly coloured clothes. 'My magical powers have brought us visitors.'

A tall man wearing what looked like a suit of armour moved forward and shouted angrily, waving a sword around alarmingly. 'Invaders more like, come to siege the castle.'

The boy shinned up the side of the balcony as agile as a cat and, looking Zack and TJ up and down warily asked, 'Well, are you invaders come to siege the castle?'

'I don't think so,' said Zack, as usual seeing the funny side of things and grinning. 'I live here, or at least I think I do.'

'Well,' said the boy, 'I really shouldn't believe you but to be honest you could get me out of a bit of a fix. The Lord and Lady down there are getting pretty bored with my magic tricks. Play along with me and I'll try and save your bacon, as well as mine.'

'Yes, I was right,' the boy called down to the knight with the sword, who was glowering suspiciously up at them. 'My magic has succeeded in bringing us a couple of travellers to entertain the Lord and Lady. I'll escort them down.'

As they descended down a long spiral staircase from the balcony to the hall, the boy turned to Zack and TJ. 'Allow me to introduce myself. I am Aric, the castle jester, and I don't know what kind of spell has brought you here, but I'm glad you came. The Lord and Lady have some knights as their guests and they are always on the lookout for a fight. I must have conjured you up, I suppose, though I do remember a story I was told years ago by my father about a strange boy who arrived at the castle back in the old years in a weird sort of cart, a magical boy who told strange tales of another time and taught my great grandfather strange and marvellous magic.'

'Probably my great uncle when he was my age,' Zack muttered.

'Time travel,' TJ explained matter of factly. 'I've read all about it. We could get stuck here, like in *Back to the Future*.'

'TJ, you don't seem to be taking this very seriously. Here, Aric, you don't think the Lord will throw us in the dungeons, do you?'

'Not unless he thinks you are spying for invaders he won't. Help me out here. If you know any tricks, use them when I tell you.'

As they reached the bottom of the stairs a crowd of knights and nobles of the castle crowded around Zack and TJ and escorted them to the Lord and Lady, who were seated in two throne-like chairs at the head of the table.

Aric hurried forward and spoke to the Lord of the castle, who conferred with some of his nobles before calling out, 'So, Aric, prove to us that these are magical beings, not spies, and let them entertain us.'

'I know lots of jokes,' said TJ, stepping forward boldly, just as Zack remembered his polaroid camera. Silently praying that it would work, he stepped forward too.

'Smile, please, ladies and gents,' he called and pressed the button. There was a bright flash and everyone shrieked with surprise, then the camera made a creaking whirring noise and a photograph shot out of the bottom. Zack held up his hand in a theatrical gesture and waited a moment as the blurred image began to clear.

It worked! Zack grinned and presented the picture to Aric, who stared at it in amazement and passed it to the Lord.

'Amazing!' declared the Lord, looking at the picture of himself and his Lady. 'A truly brilliant piece of sorcery, Aric.'

The next few hours passed by in a trice as Zack took photographs of all the nobles and their ladies and the knights as they all smiled and posed. The Lord of the castle declared that he had never had so much fun and thought Aric was terribly clever finding these travelling entertainers – whoever they were!

Zack and TJ were invited to join the feast and once they had eaten they were invited to watch a jousting competition that the knights were going to hold.

Aric took Zack and TJ to the top of a tower to get a good view and they were amazed to see how different everywhere looked.

Later, as they came down the winding stairway from the tower, the rush torch that Aric was carrying went out and they were plunged into darkness. 'Drat! We'll have to feel our way down,' Aric called back.

Suddenly the tower stairway was lit up by a small circle of bright yellow light and Aric turned to see Zack's face shining above it. 'Aaah!' he yelled, nearly tripping and tumbling backwards down the stairway.

'Hey, don't be silly, Aric, it's only a torch,' Zack called behind him, waving the beam around and laughing as Aric tried to duck away from it.

Once they were back in the brightly lit hall Aric overcame his fear and was very happy when Zack gave the torch to him, showing him how to switch it on and off.

'A present from the twentieth century, Aric,' he grinned. 'Just keep it for a special occasion. The batteries won't last forever!'

'My Lord will love this sorcery,' Aric declared happily. 'I shall save it for his next birthday celebration!'

'Well, we'd better be off now,' said TJ, glancing anxiously up to where the time-travelling dodgem car sat perched on the edge of the balcony, 'before everyone comes in from the jousting and wants us to entertain them again!'

'Still, we've had a great time, Aric,' said Zack. 'I just hope I can get us back to where we came from before we are missed.'

Once back in the dodgem car, Zack began to press buttons and pull levers, hoping it would work again. Sure enough, the car's lights began to flash and they began to hover up above the balcony, Aric waving below them. Then the car began to spin faster and faster until there was just a blur of sound and light.

Zack and TJ arrived back in the twentieth century with a splash, right in the middle of a large puddle in the castle moat. As they climbed out of the dodgem car, a little dazed and confused, and looked around them, Zack's great uncle came dashing out of the castle towards them.

'My word, Zack, you'll be the death of me,' he called out as he dashed over to them. 'However did you find that old time-machine? Your mother will be mad at me when she finds out. Still, you look okay both of you. Where did you end up then, medieval times? The useless thing is stuck on medieval, that's why I locked it away, no good at all. Come along, no harm done, eh?'

As Zack and TJ followed Zack's great-uncle back to the castle, they exchanged a quick grin.

'Look, TJ,' Zack whispered and there, sticking out of the polaroid was a picture of Aric waving goodbye.

'Just think of the history project we going to write now, eh, Zack?' said TJ, grinning.

'I can hardly wait!' Zack groaned, and the two time-travellers went wearily back into the castle . . .

Ignoring colour and just taking note of black lines – can you find the six pairs of matching squares?

How Many Boys in Our Pack?

All you have to do is count the number of boys' names in the circle.

Check your answers on page 61.

57

MAKING RECYCLED PAPER

What's so special about paper anyway?

The most important ingredient in paper is wood, and yet one whole tree can only provide enough wood for a very small amount of paper. That is why so many huge forests are being destroyed and spoiled so that we can have more and more new paper. However, there is something we can do to cut down on this wastage, by always trying to buy recycled paper and not using more paper than we really need to. Making your own recycled paper is easy and fun and means that you can help to save the environment. The next couple of pages show you, in easy step by step instructions, how to go about it.

Another idea for saving on waste paper is to refuse paper bags that may be offered to you in shops. Don't be embarrassed, after all trying to help save our planet is definitely nothing to be ashamed of, is it? Just say 'no thanks' politely and think about all the trees you'll be saving. Try taking a bag with you when you go out shopping. What about a backpack? Also, try and get Mum and Dad to take a shopping bag with them when they visit the shops and to keep the same bag to use over and over again. You could remind them every time they go to the supermarket! It is one way to cut down on the terrible waste created by all the thousands of bags that leave shops and supermarkets every day.

It isn't just bags that create waste paper though so always be on the lookout for recycled products and environmentally friendly gifts such as cards, books and writing paper (until you make some of your own!).

Best of all, be inventive, recycle old birthday and Christmas cards into gift tags, bookmarks and notelets. The list is endless once you get going!

You can use lots of different types of paper for recycling — try saving cornflake boxes, newspapers, your old comics, paper bags etc. Why not create a special place to use as a 'recycling store', maybe a spare corner of the garage or the shed, or ask if there is a kitchen cupboard or shelf you could use or even a big old box you could keep in your room. Every time someone has finished with their paper, add it to your store.

There are two ways to make your own recycled paper but if you are going to do it often (hopefully you will find this so much fun you'll want to!) then the best way is to make a paper-making frame as shown here. You can use this over and over again. There is also a quicker method which is just as effective but doesn't require a frame.

* Note: before you start, the paper used in each method needs to be soaked OVERNIGHT. You might like to do this before you begin to get all your equipment together.

A recycling frame

What you will need:

A saw
220cm (7ft) of 2.5 × 2.5cm (1 × 1in) wood
Pieces of hardboard or scrap wood 7 × 5cm (2¾ × 2in)
Sandpaper
Wood glue (non-soluble)
Hammer and 16 thin, flat-headed nails 4cm (1¾in) long
Nylon mesh or net curtain material
Scissors
Staples or drawing pins

How to make it:

Ask an adult to help you to saw the wood into eight pieces: four lengths of 30cm (12in) and four lengths of 25cm (10in). Then the scrap wood needs to be cut into four pieces: 7 × 5cm (2¾ × 2in).

Rub all the edges with sandpaper until they are smooth and then put the wood into TWO rectangles using two 30cm pieces (12in) and two 25cm (10in) pieces for each.

Make sure that all the corners are closely fitted together then glue the joints and tap a nail through each corner to make it secure.

Next, nail a piece of the scrap hardboard to the centre of one side of one of the rectangles, with two nails either side of each piece. Make sure the pieces all overhang in the same direction. This is the top section of the paper frame and is known as a deckle or cover.

If you have decided to use a piece of old netting or net curtain, first spread a thin layer of glue over the top edge of the second rectangle then wrap the piece of net over the top and glue and nail it into place, stretching it tightly as you go.

If you are using mesh, cut it to size with scissors and carefully fold under any sharp edges. Again, wrap the mesh over the second rectangle and fold the corners down neatly. Use staples or drawing pins to fasten it.

Put the frame mesh-side up and slot the first rectangle (deckle) over it so that the pieces of hardboard hold it in place.

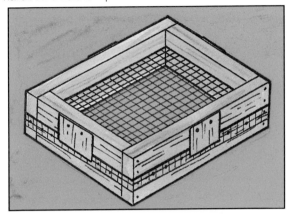

Now, if everything has gone well, you should have a paper-making frame all ready to use!

Ask an adult for the things you need before you start and make sure you wear old clothes with an old shirt or apron on top – it's easy to get covered in the stuff you are about to make!

Equipment list:

Waste paper (about 50 sheets). Computer print-out paper is best if you can get it but other types will do just as well.

Water
A bucket
Your paper frame
Washing-up liquid
An old washing-up bowl that is large enough to fit your frame in
Old potato masher
Newspaper to put where you are working
2 pieces of board (slightly larger than the frame)
About 25 old *absorbent* cloths

This is what you do:

Tear up the waste paper into 2.5cm (1in) squares. Soak the pieces overnight in a bucket of hot water – the longer it is soaked the easier it is to use. Add a little washing-up liquid to the water – this will help to remove any ink and make your finished paper look much better.

When the paper is ready to use, squeeze out fist-sized balls and put them into the washing-up bowl. Add enough water to cover.

Using the potato-masher, mix up the paper and water for about 15–20 minutes until it resembles a smooth, porridge-like paste.

Pour about half of the pulp into a bucket and then fill the washing-up bowl with the remaining pulp and about the same amount of water as before. Stir it well.

Spread a double layer of newspaper on the floor and then put one of the pieces of board on top of it. Spread a dampened piece of cloth on top of this.

Hold the paper frame, deckle-side up and then slide it, long edge first, into the washing-up bowl of diluted pulp until it is completely submerged. Swirl it gently around to spread the pulp over the surface. Lift the frame out and let it drain for a minute.

Lift the deckle off the frame then rest one long edge of the frame on the cloth and gently lower it, mesh-side down, onto the middle of the cloth.

Wipe the back of the mesh firmly with another cloth to remove as much of the water as possible.

Carefully lift the frame, starting at one corner, so that you leave the sheet of damp paper on the cloth. Cover it with another cloth.

Add about half a cup of pulp from the bucket to the mixture in the washing-up bowl and stir it up well. Make another sheet of paper and lay it on top of the previous cloth. Carry on layering the paper and cloths until all the mixture is used up.

Place the second piece of board on top of the last cloth and then gently stand on top of it to squeeze all the water out. Be careful though, don't jump up and down!

In a warm room, cover a table with newspaper to keep it dry. Remove the top board and cloth and then carefully lay out each sheet of paper (still attached to its cloth) face up on the table. Leave for a few hours until the cloths are dry but the paper is still a little damp.

Turn each sheet over and carefully peel off the cloth and then leave to dry completely.

To smooth the paper even more, press it with a cool iron when dry.

The quick and easy way:

Equipment:

Old newspaper   A wooden spoon or a liquidizer   Absorbent cloths   Wire mesh

A bucket and a shallow bowl   A plastic bag   Weights, e.g. heavy books

How to make it:

Soak the old newspaper overnight in a bowl or bucket. Then drain off the excess water and use either a wooden spoon or a liquidizer to mash the paper and water into a pulp. Make sure the lid is on the liquidizer if you use one!

Put the pulp into another bowl and add an equal volume of water. Mix the two together well and slide the wire mesh into the mixture. Then, carefully lift out the mesh, which should be covered in pulp.

Lay a cloth on a clean flat surface and quickly place the mesh, pulp-side down, onto the cloth. Press it down hard, then peel it off, leaving the pulp on the cloth. Put another cloth on top and press down firmly.

Continue to layer the mixture with the cloths in this way until it is all used up and then place the plastic bag on the top and cover with weights.

Leave to dry for several hours and the mixture will turn to paper. Gently peel it away from the cloths and leave it flat on some newspaper or paper towels until it is completely dry and ready to use!

Answers

Jungle Book Maze (Page 4)

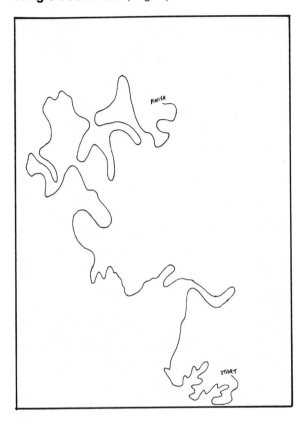

What are the Activity Badges? (Page 16)

1. Handyman, 2. Local Historian, 3. Athlete no 2.

Cub Scouting Wordsearch (Page 32)

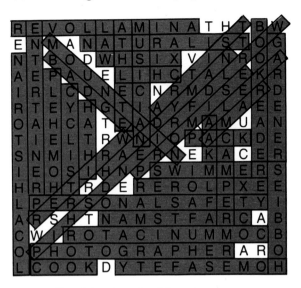

Answer: The Adventure Crest Award.

Wildlife Acrostic (Page 35)

Wasp, tapir, curlew, vulture, python, heron, slug = WARTHOG.

Square Pairs (Page 57)

B2–E5, B5–C1, C6–E7, B6–C3, A4–E2, A2–A5.

How Many Boys in our Pack? (Page 57)

There are 22 boys – Brian, Anthony, Yule, Leonard, Donald, Aldous, Sebastian, Ian, Neil, Laurence, Cecil, Luke, Kevin, Vincent, Terence, Cedric, Richard, Daniel, Elmer, Eric, Cuthbert and Bert.

Continued from page 31

Ice Cream Monster

A block of ice cream for each monster, any colour or flavour.
Any of the following:
Chocolate buttons
Sugar-coated chocolate beans
Chocolate twigs
Hundreds and thousands
Cherries
Jam or raspberry sauce
Shredded coconut
Toasted almond bits
Liquorice bits
Ice cream wafers or cones

Or anything else that takes your fancy! It's often best to think of what kind of monsters you are going to make before you buy some of the ingredients.
Also:
A pallet knife
Fish slice
Two plates (these need to be really cold so put them in the fridge or freezer for a little while before you start)
Knife and fork

Cut the ice cream into the basic shape that you want on one plate and then lift it with the fish slice on to the other. Using any leftover ice cream, add heads, tails, legs, feet etc, or use a different coloured ice cream for contrast.

Then comes the really fun part! Decorate the monster in whatever way you like. Use the sweets, nuts and cherries for eyes or lumpy skin, chocolate twigs for spikes or fangs with red sauce dripping from them! Try ideas like a chocolate swamp monster with green jelly spots (sweets) all over it, a vanilla robot with liquorice sweets for bolts and joints, or a strawberry spikey monster with chocolate spikes. Anything goes!

As soon as you have made your monster as gruesome as possible, eat it! Or put it in the fridge or freezer until you are ready.

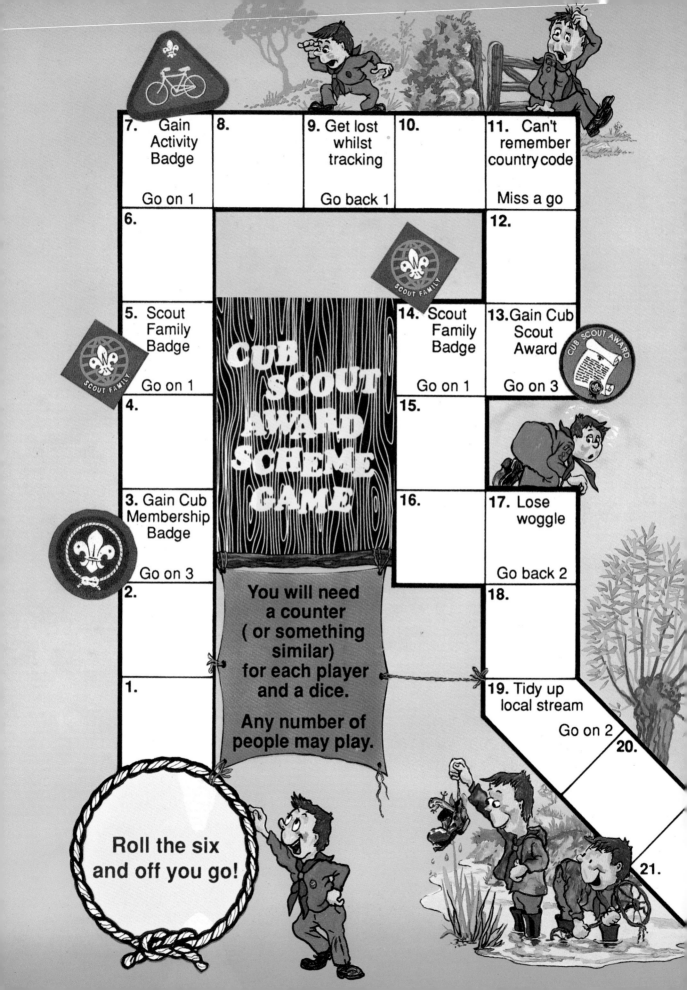

7. Gain Activity Badge Go on 1	8.	9. Get lost whilst tracking Go back 1	10.	11. Can't remember country code Miss a go
6.				12.
5. Scout Family Badge Go on 1			14. Scout Family Badge Go on 1	13. Gain Cub Scout Award Go on 3
4.			15.	
3. Gain Cub Membership Badge Go on 3			16.	17. Lose woggle Go back 2
2.				18.
1.				19. Tidy up local stream Go on 2

CUB SCOUT AWARD SCHEME GAME

You will need a counter (or something similar) for each player and a dice.

Any number of people may play.

Roll the six and off you go!

20.

21.